The Dilemma
of Reform
in the
Soviet Union

The Dilemma of Reform in the Soviet Union

Timothy J. Colton

COUNCIL ON FOREIGN RELATIONS, INC.
58 East 68 Street, New York NY 10021

COUNCIL ON FOREIGN RELATIONS BOOKS

The Council on Foreign Relations, Inc., is a nonprofit and nonpartisan organization devoted to promoting improved understanding of international affairs through the free exchange of ideas. The Council does not take any position on questions of foreign policy and has no affiliation with, and receives no funding from, the United States government.

From time to time, books and monographs written by members of the Council's research staff or visiting fellows, or commissioned by the Council, or written by an independent author with critical review contributed by a Council study or working group are published with the designation "Council on Foreign Relations Book." Any book or monograph bearing that designation is, in the judgment of the Committee on Studies of the Council's board of directors, a responsible treatment of a significant international topic worthy of presentation to the public. All statements of fact and expressions of opinion contained in Council books are, however, the sole responsibility of the author.

Printed in the United States of America

Library of Congress Cataloging in Publication Data

Colton, Timothy J., 1947–
   The dilemma of reform in the Soviet Union.

   Includes bibliographical references.
   1. Heads of state--Soviet Union--Succession.
2. Soviet Union--Politics and government--1953–
I. Title.
JN6540.C64 1984   947.085'3   84-9587
ISBN 0-87609-002-1

Contents

Foreword

For the Soviet Union the 1980s seem certain to be a difficult and challenging interlude. Two political successions have already occurred, and at least one more is likely before the decade is out. As one leader fast follows another, the regime must cope with an increasingly trying agenda of economic and social problems. Steadily declining economic growth rates, labor shortages, deteriorating worker morale, and ethnic frictions constitute but a part of the list.

It is often not easy, however, for the outside observer to gauge how serious these problems are, what they add up to when taken together, and how the Soviet leadership is likely to respond to them. The Council on Foreign Relations has turned to Timothy J. Colton to provide this kind of broad, ultimate judgment, with a general audience in mind. His essay grew out of a 1982–83 Council study group on the Soviet Union's problems and the prospects for internal reform, led by Professor Samuel P. Huntington. In exploring a wide range of issues — from the role of the military to relations among nationality groups, from younger politicians' rise to the economy's decline — the group heard from an array of experts: Jeremy Azrael, Seweryn Bialer, George Breslauer, Zbigniew Brzezinski, Gail Warshofsky Lapidus, Herbert Levine, William E. Odom, Richard Pipes, Dimitri Simes, and Douglas Whitehouse.

The analysis in this essay, however, is very much Professor Colton's own. We think the reader will find in its relatively few pages an accessible, comprehensive, and stimulating exploration of the tough agenda confronting General Secretary Chernenko, his colleagues, and their heirs.

Paul Kreisberg
Director of Studies

Robert Legvold
Senior Fellow

Preface

The death of Leonid Brezhnev on November 10, 1982, closed a chapter of Soviet history exceptional for its stability and predictability. Now, with difficulties mounting on several fronts, little can be taken for granted about the country's prospects by the Soviet public or by foreign onlookers. One new General Secretary, Yuri Andropov, has died after only fifteen months in office, and a second interim leader, Konstantin Chernenko, has been installed. Some have likened the Soviet Union's current uncertainty to the aftermath of Stalin's death thirty years ago, or even to the "times of troubles," those interregnums between eras of firm and settled government found in earlier Russian history. By a variety of yardsticks, the problems besetting the Soviet regime have worsened in recent years. At the same time, the elite ruling the USSR is in unusual flux. A displacement of governing teams and generations throughout the party and state, of which the accessions of Andropov and Chernenko constitute but one episode, is well under way and should be complete within less than a decade.

The present essay aims to make developments within the Soviet Union during this phase of transition intelligible to the lay reader. It argues that the internal course most likely to be taken over the next five or ten years is one of moderate reform. This is not a cheap exit from the regime's present predicament. Reform is a complex dilemma for the Soviet leaders: a strategy to which they turn with great reluctance and which is fraught with difficulties and contradictions of its own. Chapter 1 begins by summarizing the ambiguous record of Brezhnev's eighteen years in power. Chapter 2 takes stock of the main problems, chief among them economic problems, now on the agenda of a changing leadership. Chapter 3 treats the succession struggle and the larger trends within the Soviet elite. The heart of the essay is Chapter 4, which presents the case for moderate reform as the most tenable of the Soviet system's several options and suggests what kinds of changes it would call for. Chapter 5 broadens the discussion to consider the links between Soviet domestic events and the world outside.

It is important to nail down key terms at the outset. The Soviet Union's political choices can be placed on a left-right spectrum corresponding roughly to the alternatives facing any society. At the left-hand pole is *revolution,* which brings about fundamental, rapid, and violent change. *Reform* involves improvement and change, but promoted by gradual and peaceful means. *Conservatism* simply preserves the status quo and keeps change in abeyance. And *reaction,* at the right end of the spectrum, embodies backward change, a restoration of some previously lost state of affairs.

Reform, the option most central to this monograph, bands together a wide range of actions and styles. It is useful, therefore, to differentiate among three types of reform. *Radical reform* is the closest to revolution: all-encompassing change containing as an essential component the restructuring of the country's political institutions and central, legitimating beliefs and myths. *Minimal reform,* at the conservative extreme, entails minor adjustments of policy and practice designed to cause the least possible disruption and conflict. *Moderate reform* is the most likely course for the near Soviet future, and it takes in the middle zone between radical and minimal reform. The moderate reformer, as distinct from the radical reformer, does not set out to remake his society's basic political structures and traditions. His target is the more modest one of government policy and implementing machinery. But, in contrast to the minimal reformer, the changes he effects here are recognized as major departures, not marginal ones. Working selectively within the existing institutional framework, the purveyor of moderate reform self-consciously alters the way rewards and privileges are allocated in society. He accepts that one price of doing so will be open conflict over his program.

One more preliminary point must be made, and that is that politicians in the Soviet Union as elsewhere do not always display the consistency that the authors of definitions do. It often happens that a government or political movement pursues elements of several different strategies simultaneously. The Brezhnev leadership did this, hewing essentially to a conservative line but also dabbling in reaction and minimal reform. The new Soviet rulers do not confront the kind of all-or-nothing choice sometimes imagined by Western observers: transformation or degeneration, change or paralysis, reform or repression, and so forth. A strategy of moderate reform would in all likelihood amalgamate significant changes of policy with conservatism on some important issues and perhaps reaction on others, and it would make extensive use of unreformed, authoritarian methods. Most Westerners would not have an easy time fathoming such a solution. This makes it doubly imperative to think through why it may appeal to the new men in the Kremlin and what it would mean for the Soviet people and the USSR's place in the world.

Acknowledgments

I am pleased to record not a few debts incurred in the preparation of this essay. The first is to Robert Legvold of the Council on Foreign Relations, who first involved me in the project and contributed enormously as sounding board, critic, and editor to the writing of the monograph. I also benefited greatly from the presentations and discussion in the Council study group. For reading of draft chapters, ideas, and access to unpublished research, I am deeply grateful to Seweryn Bialer, George Breslauer, Lawrence Caldwell, Barbara Chotiner, Alexander Dallin, Paul Goble, Thane Gustafson, Werner Hahn, Jerry Hough, Ellen Jones, Paul Kreisberg, Robbin Laird, Gail Warshofsky Lapidus, T. H. Rigby, Blair Ruble, Strobe Talbott, and the Council's two anonymous referees. Andrea Zwiebel of the Council on Foreign Relations staff gave excellent technical support. And, finally, the Kennan Institute for Advanced Russian Studies of the Woodrow Wilson International Center for Scholars in Washington, D.C., provided a hospitable setting where most of the original draft was completed.

Timothy J. Colton

University of Toronto, April 1984

1

Brezhnev's Ambiguous Legacy

The Brezhnev Leadership Style

Leonid Ilyich Brezhnev held power eighteen years and twenty-seven days, longer than any Soviet leader except Stalin. To his immediate heirs, Yuri Andropov and Konstantin Chernenko, he left a legacy of accomplishments but also of challenges and looming problems. For the younger politicians who will soon step into their shoes, the Brezhnev years were a crucial formative experience. The triumphs and failures of this period will have a major effect on Soviet politics for the balance of this century.

Brezhnev's legacy defies easy analysis. Andropov is said to have "grasped well the Brezhnevite (*brezhnevskii*) style of leadership, the Brezhnevite concern for the people's interests, the Brezhnevite attitude toward personnel," but this is a hymn less to Brezhnev the man than to the era over which he presided.[1] By the standards of the Soviet past, Brezhnev's rule was curiously impersonal. Lenin was a revolutionary, Stalin a despot, and Khrushchev a flawed reformer, to follow the simple labels of Western textbooks. But what was Brezhnev? What did he stand for, and what did he leave behind?

Part of the puzzle arises from the character and mind-set of Brezhnev himself. Sketchy evidence suggests that he was a person of breadth rather than depth, more a tactician than a strategist, superficially voluble but reticent and cautious on the points that counted. Before reaching the top in October 1964, Brezhnev had been everything from farm laborer to agricultural administrator, metallurgical engineer, and municipal official, and eventually to military commissar, regional party viceroy, Central Committee overseer of defense production and the space program, titular head of the Soviet state, and party secretary in charge of personnel. His career took him to several parts of the Ukraine and to Belorussia, the Urals, Moldavia, and Kazakhstan before settling him in Moscow. As General Secretary of

1

the Communist Party, Brezhnev remained in many respects an elusive and enigmatic figure. His quirks and endearing gestures were few, and they were better known outside the Soviet Union than inside. He did have policy preoccupations—such as the building of Soviet military might and the modernization of agriculture—but even these he touted like someone reading the minutes of a committee meeting.

Brezhnev's ghost-written memoirs betray no hint of inner drives or anxieties and reinforce the impression of a stolid individual accustomed more to accommodating to his surroundings than actively molding them. Among his few personal remarks are limp eulogies of his father, from whom he had inherited "stubbornness, patience, and the habit, once having started something, of without fail carrying it through to its conclusion," and of his mother, from whom he had learned "amiability, interest in people, and the knack of meeting trouble with a smile or joke."[2] People who had known the rule of his predecessors were both reassured and amused by such pale sentimentality and by the sight of Brezhnev in his square-cut suits and oversized neckties, laboriously reciting speeches from note cards on the evening television news. Brezhnev provoked neither strong affection nor strong antipathy. My many attempts to draw Soviet acquaintances into conversation about him discovered little knowledge and less interest.

To assess the murky nature of the Brezhnev era, we must return to the politics that carried him to power. The 1964 palace revolt against Nikita Khrushchev was in the simplest political terms a repudiation of Khrushchev's highly personalized operating mode, his penchant for riding roughshod over the opinions of the inner circle and those serving under them. If Stalin, who possessed more potent instruments of tyranny, could get away with this, Khrushchev could not. Having emptied most of the labor camps and foresworn mass terror, he was dictator enough to alienate his fellow governors but not to cow them. His successors, once they had safely relegated Khrushchev to his *dacha*, in effect wrote a "charter of oligarchy" for the Soviet system, entrenching collective leadership at its summit.[3] In the process they split off Khrushchev's office as head of government—that is, Chairman of the Council of Ministers—and awarded it to a second major figure within the Politburo, Aleksei Kosygin.

Over time Brezhnev slowly amended this charter of oligarchy in his favor. By the late 1970s, he appeared bedecked with medals and ribbons, his memoirs were printed in huge editions and given state prizes, a patchy Brezhnev war record was being extolled, and he had been named Chairman of the Presidium of the Supreme Soviet, or ceremonial head of state. Nevertheless, even as his power grew, along with the stilted Brezhnev cult, his associates applauded him most for fostering team decision making. "One of the best qualities of Leonid Ilyich," the Georgian first secretary stated in 1976, "lies in the fact that he does not don the mantle of a superman, that he does not think and work for everyone but, while making his own outstanding contribution to the common cause, creates the conditions under which all can think creatively." This and other tributes were inspired most by the things Brezhnev did not do. He did not affect omniscience, he did not push others around, he did not sow "blind fear, egoism, envy, or suspicion."[4] At a mawkish seventy-fifth birthday celebration in December 1981 (his last), Brezhnev returned to the theme of collaborative leadership. The strides made since 1964 were not his alone, he said, but the product of "true mutual understanding in the leadership . . . the practice of joint investigation and serious discussion . . . and the joint taking of decisions."[5]

If Brezhnevism resists simple characterization, therefore, this reflects the political settlement around which it was fashioned. Especially in the early years, power at the top was divided and shared. And the kingpin of the regime was temperamentally suited to its bland image and far less gripped than previous bosses by strong ideas that he wished to impose on Soviet society.

The Three Faces of Brezhnevism

A more fundamental factor obstructs an easy assessment of the Brezhnev period. Whatever is said about power relations and personalities, we are left with a chronicle of action that is complex and less than fully consistent. The leadership followed not one but three basic lines of domestic policy—conservative, reactionary, and timidly reformist—and among these there was both overlap and contradiction.

Conservatism was, without much doubt, the foremost of the three strands. The leadership under Brezhnev wanted most to give the USSR a regime of stability and balance after the turbulence of the Khrushchev years. Its conservative bent was clearest in the area of personnel. To the thousands of office-holders who make up the Soviet political machine, Brezhnevism translated above all into a novel job security. Turnover at all levels was unhurried: changes within the Politburo took place at a third of the rate of the Khrushchev period, and membership in the Central Committee "almost took on the appearance of a life peerage."[6] Promotions were put on a more orderly footing, as replacements now came chiefly from within the given region or agency. The contrast was stark both with Khrushchev, who hired and fired freely on the basis of policy and whim, and with Stalin, at whose hands demotion was an ever-lurking danger and could mean instant disgrace or death. This convention of "respect for cadres," as it came to be known, had a corollary: "trust in cadres," which signified the enlarging of officials' authority and leeway in carrying out their functions. This Brezhnev justified on good conservative grounds, as an expression of faith in the human products of the Soviet system: "It has been a long time since there grew up in our midst qualified cadres, able to resolve correctly all the questions falling within their competence. We must trust them more and accordingly make them responsible for more."[7]

A reflexive conservatism was equally evident when it came to institutions and ideology. Khrushchev had treated the units of the party apparatus and economic bureaucracy like building blocks that he could stack at will to suit the slogans and enthusiasms of the hour. Within months of his fall, most of his restructurings were erased and an indefinite moratorium was declared on big reorganizations. Similarly, the flow of doctrinal invention was reduced to a trickle. "Developed socialism," the new catchphrase for Soviet reality, exuded self-satisfaction, and Brezhnevite propaganda gave pride of place to the symbols of order and stability standard to conservative regimes everywhere: patriotism, duty, family, army, the benevolent state. Active measures were taken to nullify ideological challenges, especially from groups urging a more liberal stance toward intellectual and cultural self-expression. Trial and the camps, police intimidation and smear tactics, and exile eventually silenced almost all the leading Soviet dissidents. In the same key, Soviet tanks were used in 1968 to smother the radical reforms begun by Alexander Dubček's Czechoslovak regime; the threat of Soviet invasion contributed to the crushing of Solidarity in Poland thirteen years later.

Equally conservative was the Brezhnev leadership's basic attitude toward making public policies. From the beginning, it espoused what was phrased a "scientific approach" to, and "scientific management" of, concrete problems. Policy was to be set after scrupulous planning and testing—the antithesis of Khrushchev's brainstorms and crusades—in conformity with clear procedures. There was to be close consultation with the established authorities in the area, among whom the regime numbered not only officials in the government, party, and military hierarchies but scientifically and technically trained specialists outside the bureaucracy. Brezhnev thought enough of the specialists' role to endorse it in his first major speech as head of the party, saying that the regime should "treasure" them and "rely on their knowledge and experience."[8] As in other countries, deference to bureaucrats and specialists tended to produce narrowly-focused decisions, not bold departures from established policy. Unless the Politburo had strong preconceptions about a problem, experts were left to themselves to thrash out disputes through analysis and bargaining, with a minimum of interference from on high.

A prime beneficiary of the leadership's conservatism and aversion to risk was the Soviet military establishment, the ultimate guarantor of the security of the regime and its foreign clients. Military spending, which Brezhnev liked to refer to as a "sacred duty" of the party, grew at a steady 4 to 5 percent a year until 1977 when, according to U.S. Central Intelligence Agency figures released in the autumn of 1983, the rate of increase slowed to about 2 percent. Besides the comprehensive buildup of strategic and conventional forces, the regime extended the civil defense program, instituted basic military training in the secondary schools, and imposed a regimen of "military-patriotic education" on the mass media, youth, and sports organizations. Beginning in 1973, a seat in the party Politburo was reserved for the Minister of Defense.

If stand-pat conservatism was the cornerstone of Brezhnevism, it by no means made up the whole structure. Some of the regime's actions went beyond preservation of the status quo to outright reaction, working to turn the clock back. One major reactionary policy was the cutting-short of the de-Stalinization pressed by Khrushchev and the partial refurbishing of Stalin's reputation, mostly as wartime leader. Rehabilitated in much the same way was the Soviet security police, the KGB, whose scope of activity, prestige, and representation in decision organs were all gradually increased under Brezhnev.[9] Without this, the coming to power in 1982 of a long-time KGB chief, Andropov, who in 1973 had become the first head of that organizaton to be elevated to the Politburo since Stalin's day, would have been unthinkable.

The incessant campaign to glorify the epic victory in World War II was another backward-looking policy. Leonid Brezhnev, its most ardent champion, seemed at some moments almost to want to bring the days of heroism and sacrifice back to life: "The war ended long ago, but in our memory there sound the voices of our fallen dear ones, our friends, our brother soldiers. We see their faces, our hands feel their firm handshakes, we remember what they talked about and what we dreamed of together."[10] More generally, official and popular interest in Russian history, folklore, and art reached a new crescendo during Brezhnev's term of office. Russia's wars, countryside, and traditional mores were the subject of many of the most lauded novels and films, and a similar quickening of interest in the past occurred in the non-Russian communities. A year never went by without the extravagant observance in Moscow of at least one big political or institutional anniversary. The regnant mood was one of nostalgia, of a quest, as one aged army marshal put it in 1981, for bridges "to connect the past with the present, yesterday with tomorrow."[11]

It would be wrong to make too much of these retreats. The reinstatement of Stalin, as an example, was incomplete in that it sidestepped his crimes and purges, the victims of which continued slowly to be exonerated.

In 1969 the Politburo expressly rejected a bid by pro-Stalin forces in the party and the arts to whitewash his entire career.[12] The KGB, although also boosted in status, remained under tight party control, never regaining its place under Stalin as a predatory state within a state. Repugnant though its present operations may be, they are a far cry from the horrors of the earlier era, when the secret police murdered citizens and banished them to Siberia almost as a normal constabulary hands out traffic tickets. Likewise with the veneration of the Russian heritage: while it was willingly patronized by the government, extreme versions were denied financial support and chastised in official writings.

By and large, the reactionary side of Brezhnevism reinforced its core conservatism. But how did these two qualities fit with a third, namely, Brezhnev's circumscribed reformism? There is no question that the Brezhnev leadership looked askance at radical reform, shunning even the moderate reforms of the ebullient Khrushchev. Nevertheless, it did originate or tolerate a great many minimal reforms—piecemeal policy changes intended to ease specific problems or allay the frustrations of particular groups in the establishment without seriously altering the system.

The basically conservative instincts of Brezhnev's coalition coexisted uneasily with this third tendency. Even so, Brezhnev's stabilizing policies, and a few of his reactionary ones as well, at times tallied surprisingly well with the spirit of minimal reform. Thus, certain backward-looking cultural trends maturing in the 1970s—the restoration of old buildings, the romanticization of traditional village life in movies and books, and the fortified boom in World War II lore, to name several—were welcomed by many Soviets. Though past-oriented, to the average person these adjustments amounted to a kind of reform.[13] The same can be said of the regime's more reassuring personnel policy. As one Western student of it has noted, to the extent that the new leaders' mentality pushed them to scrap the essentially Stalinist practices of arbitrary dismissal of officials and capricious redefinition of their duties, they in their own fashion "pushed the reform of Stalinism further than Khrushchev did."[14]

A similarly balanced verdict should be rendered on the oligarchy's conservative partiality for "scientific" determination of social and economic policies. This position, and the mobilization of experts accompanying it, had a settling effect on government policy, avoiding the gyrations and "harebrained schemes" over which Khrushchev came to grief. By the same token, the new-found preoccupation with knowledge, rationality, and the "scientific-technological revolution" made the authorities more amenable to temperate, problem-solving change within the confines of the existing order.

One of the regime's first acts was to disavow Trofim Lysenko, the vicious charlatan who, with backing in the Kremlin, had warped Soviet biology and agricultural science since the late 1940s and on whose behalf Khrushchev had blustered about dismantling the revered Academy of Sciences. Lysenko's fall was seen by the intelligentsia as a signal that ham-handed political meddling in the work of competent and loyal specialists was to be curtailed.[15] This and other new guidelines had the potent side-effect of accelerating the movement begun in Khrushchev's time toward fuller public airing of policy questions. After 1964 the political elbowroom of the skilled professional was greatly expanded in nearly every field of policy.[16] Politicians could still veto change, declare ultrasensitive matters out of bounds, and control the way ideas were expressed. Yet, the richer and blunter discussion of policy issues, big and small, should impress anyone reading Soviet publications of the day. Advisers in many fields were permitted and urged to do public opinion surveys and incorporate the results (which were not always published) into their recommendations. Ironically, the same regime that locked dissidents in psychiatric hospitals and outlawed proposals for radical change also countenanced the most candid debate seen in Soviet Russia since the 1920s on a host of within-system issues: in the economic sphere, on questions of planning, investment, man-power, energy, trade and technology transfer, and technical innovation; on institutional questions, the relative powers of central and local agencies, the handling of citizens' complaints, and the role of the trade unions; in the social area, problems of crime, pollution, the needs of the elderly and of working women, the difficulties of declining villages and of metropolitan areas; or simply on aspects of life style such as family size, alcoholism, and the effects of television.[17]

Brezhnev's specific policy choices also reflect a good deal of pragmatic innovation. They involved "marginal adjustments, evolving experiments, and creeping innovations within the system," not abrupt breaks with precedent, but their cumulative significance cannot be denied.[18] Soviet environmental policy, for instance, was gingerly altered under Brezhnev. Following lengthy debate, the regime in the 1970s enacted more than fifty pieces of national legislation on pollution control. It also made city planning and construction more responsive to local climate, topography, and tastes.

The minimal reforms Brezhnev most prized were those directly benefiting the Soviet consumer. Compared to Khrushchev (to say nothing of Stalin), the Brezhnev administration "demonstrated greater pragmatism in confronting the consumer sector [and] greater willingness to disregard the ideological implications of consumerism."[19] In the second half of the 1960s, spurred by budgetary reallocations and entreaties that heavy industry manufacture more consumer goods, per capita consumption surged by over 5 percent a year, a postwar zenith for the Soviet Union. Between 1970 and

1980, although rates of growth of consumption tapered off, they sufficed to lift the percentage of Soviet families owning refrigerators from 32 to 86, television sets from 51 to 83, washing machines from 52 to 70, and cars from 2 to 9.[20] From his first months in office, the General Secretary threw his political weight behind an unprecedented drive to enlarge food production. Agriculture's share of total investment in the economy was increased from 20 to 27 percent (it is 7 or 8 percent in the United States), as the better part of one trillion rubles was expended on irrigation, land reclamation, electrification, farm machinery, and the like. The bulk of new production was used to feed livestock and put more meat on the Soviet family's table. For the first time, the regime also committed itself (after the poor 1972 harvest) to routine purchases of immense amounts of foreign-grown grain, both to make up for shortfalls in bad crop years and to allow quicker startup of the livestock-raising program. In the period 1976–81 alone, Soviet longshoremen unloaded 69.4 million tons of corn and 64.2 million tons of wheat bought on the world market, about 40 percent of it from the United States.[21]

In social policy, the Brezhnev leadership continued the trend toward egalitarianism begun under Khrushchev. The spread in earnings was shrunk further, as wages were hiked at the bottom of the scale and virtually frozen at the upper end.[22] The prices of most foodstuffs, consumer staples, housing, and transportation were held constant, a practice that favored the more poorly paid. Meanwhile, farm incomes, traditionally much lower than urban incomes, were raised more rapidly than the average; and Soviet peasants were brought fully into the social security web, given pension and other benefits previously unavailable to them. And, in 1974, the leadership started a special program to relieve the impoverished state of central Russia's non-black-earth zone.

In the field of economic management, the Brezhnev Politburo in 1965 decreed the introduction of price and profit incentives but within the framework of centralized planning. This shilly-shallying proved unpopular with the bureaucracy and unworkable in practice and was shelved in the early 1970s. Thereafter, the leadership continued to be receptive to economic and socioeconomic experiments at the level of the individual plant or locality. Some examples were the effort to reduce industrial overmanning begun at the Shchekino Chemical Combine in 1967; the city employment bureaus, implicitly acknowledging the problem posed by the misallocation of manpower, launched in Ufa and Kaluga in 1971; the "social planning" movement in large enterprises and cities, which tied productivity to improvements in the work environment and social services; and the shift toward local government control of housing construction pioneered in Orel in 1972. The regime gave these ventures its blessing, recommended their general adoption, and called for further experimentation.

The Soviet system was also opened up to the outside world by the Brezhnev leadership. Trade with the capitalist countries, touched off under Khrushchev in the 1950s, continued and deepened. Bolstered by détente and the windfall profits from Moscow's oil and gold sales in the 1970s, trade with the West reached a third of the Soviet total by the end of the decade. Aggressive buying abroad contributed advanced Western machinery and technology to the modernization of Soviet industry. Along the way, direct and indirect contacts with foreign, especially Western, ideas and personnel were multiplied and a large domestic constituency with a strong thirst for more contact was created. Soviet ideas on management science and related questions were brought into the international mainstream, despite "bureaucratic lethargy and even fierce resistance from conservative forces in the Soviet establishment."[23]

Stereotypes to the contrary, there were also modest reforms in the area of individual liberties. The rough and methodical (though almost never lethal) suppression of cultural and political dissent was one side to regime policy. Equally a part of the picture was the relaxation of controls over not a few other facets of Soviet life. The government greatly moderated the Khrushchev-era persecution of religion, the harassment of private production and sale of food, and the pressure for conformity in matters such as dress and hair style. The five-day work week, instituted in the late 1960s, added leisure time for the industrial work force. In a move predicted by almost no one, some 400,000 Soviet citizens, mostly Jews, Germans, and Armenians, were grudgingly permitted to emigrate, numbers unheard of since shortly after the Russian Revolution. Communication with relatives and friends outside the Soviet bloc was much eased, and there was a letup in the jamming of foreign radio broadcasts. While censorship in literature remained strict, state fetters were perceptibly loosened in some of the other arts, including cinema, music (especially popular music), and architecture.

The Loss of Vigor and Direction

Brezhnev's policies were an alloy of conservatism, reaction, and muted reformism. His Politburo was neither a collection of cardboard villains nor, as it was caricatured by some in the West in the late 1960s, a "regime of clerks."[24] As originally conceived, Brezhnev's conservatism was flexible and adaptive. What is more, for some time it worked tolerably well. Brezhnev could announce on the occasion of his seventieth birthday in December 1976 — probably the high-water mark of the regime's optimism — that "never before over the length of its entire history has our country enjoyed such authority and influence in the world." The Soviet Union had achieved nuclear parity with the United States and détente with the West, maintained its imperial holdings in Eastern Europe, and acquired new toeholds in the

Third World. At home, Brezhnev could talk with some reason of "great things accomplished . . . under the leadership of the party" since his accession.[25] Communist rule seemed more impregnable than ever. The regime's mix of policies was widely accepted among the population and strategic elites, and Brezhnev was spared the ignominy that had betided his predecessor.

It is fair to say that the smugness voiced by Brezhnev in 1976 died before he did. The closing years of his administration were not happy ones. They were marked by reverses, disappointments, and self-doubts. Clues of declining effectiveness were showing up by the early 1970s. The disastrous 1975 harvest and, in foreign relations, the skirmish with the United States over Angola were still thought by many Soviets to have been isolated events. In fact, they foretold a more general onset of difficulties later in the decade. Some of these flowed from simple bad luck—the foul weather beginning in 1979, for example, which helped send agricultural output tumbling for four straight years, or the sag in oil and gold prices after 1980, costing the Soviets billions in foreign exchange. Others represented the failure of specific policy gambles—for instance, in the early 1970s that the railway system could handle heavier traffic without expensive modernization, an error leading to mammoth transport snarls a decade later. And yet, what is most striking about the troubles of the late Brezhnev years is how wide-ranging they were. They flared up in foreign policy (the demise of U.S.-Soviet détente, the army mired in Afghanistan, the revolt in Poland), too, but most glaringly in domestic affairs. Here there was ample reason by the time of Brezhnev's death to gather that more than mishap and bad bets was involved, that some quite basic formulas were no longer working. How critical these underlying problems are will be considered in the following chapter.

In evaluating Brezhnev, however, it should be remembered that he piloted the Soviet Union through ten or twelve years of comparative prosperity and tranquility. He will be faulted by historians less for any single decision than for an inability to alter compass as previously uncharted reefs and shoals came into view. What with the workings of political cronyism and the aging process, any such shift of course would have been most unlikely. As deaths and the odd demotion thinned the ranks of the original leadership, the substitutes frequently were mediocre types picked for their earlier associations with Brezhnev. When a dying Kosygin retired in 1980, his replacement as Chairman of the Council of Ministers, an illustrious office once held by Lenin and Stalin, was Nikolai Tikhonov, a nondescript, seventy-five-year-old functionary whose one essential qualification was his having worked with Brezhnev in the Dnepropetrovsk region of the Ukraine three decades earlier. Konstantin Chernenko, a member of Brezhnev's entourage since the early 1950s, and for a long spell his personal aide, was made a national party secretary in 1976 and a Politburo member in 1978 (at age sixty-seven). From 1966 to 1981 the average age of full members of the Politburo advanced by twelve years, from fifty-eight to seventy, something helped by the leadership's failure for the first time in fifty-four years to make a single change in Politburo membership at the Twenty-sixth Party Congress in 1981. The effects of senescence were most cruelly apparent in Brezhnev himself. From 1975 onward, he experienced alternating bouts of illness and semi-recuperation (toward the end, so the Moscow rumor mill said, aided by the ministrations of a faith healer). By his last several years, he was an enfeebled and pathetic figure, a part-time patriarch who had difficulty speaking, hearing, and remembering and who, some of the Soviet foreign policy establishment claim, was given to emotional breakdowns, with outbursts of weeping, in the course of ordinary Politburo sessions.

The leadership's political vigor was hardly greater. As a result, from the mid-1970s forward the balance among the three basic tendencies of policy tilted strongly in favor of plain conservatism. Reforms, even minimal reforms, require a search for alternative courses of action and an energetic execution of the decisions already arrived at. At the pinnacle of the Soviet system, and indeed throughout high officialdom, curiosity and energy became increasingly scarce commodities. While straightforward redirections of capital could still be accomplished — witness the crash campaign to develop Siberian natural gas for export to Western Europe in the early 1980s — decisions breaking new ground became more and more rare. As for the partial reforms of earlier years, less and less effort was made to follow through on them. Mildly auspicious experiments in economic and social management languished in various provincial backwaters, their authors learning the hard way that a stray kind word in a *Pravda* editorial or a Brezhnev speech was not enough. In the absence of top-level support, each challenge to bureaucratic inertia "had to be guided through so great an amount of paperwork as to drive out the taste for changes of even the most optimistically inclined executives. . . . The enthusiasm of many supporters was extinguished by the wave of paper."[26]

There is much to indicate that concern over the country's loss of direction and momentum was building in the late Brezhnev era. One need look no further than the public remarks of Brezhnev himself, who gave signs of having developed second thoughts about certain of his commitments without acquiring the stomach for changing them. Some of his most agitated comments were directed at the very compact underpinning his regime: the commitment to "respect" and "trust" its officials. In November 1979, in the sharpest Brezhnev speech ever made public, he complained of do-nothing officials who would never change, "no matter how much you speak to them, how much you appeal to their conscience or sense of duty." It was time, he said, "to replace those who cannot cope with their assigned work," and "more freely to promote energetic and creatively thinking comrades, [people] with initiative." Eleven members of the Council of Ministers were criticized by name. It was the kind of threat not heard since Khrushchev's day.[27]

Brezhnev also noted the regime's failure to implement well-thought-out decisions. As early as 1976 he was deploring the fact that "certain decisions, on account of weak control, are either not carried out or are carried out imprecisely or incompletely." Second or third resolutions were sometimes merely tacked onto the first, he added, and all of them left unfulfilled. In later addresses, Brezhnev conveyed increasing exasperation: "Comrades, I am probably telling you things you already know, but [here Brezhnev resorted to an expression most often used in the classroom] repetition is the mother of learning (*povtoreniye — mat' ucheniya*)." From time to time there was the implied fear that the results would be calamitous if the situation, especially in the economy, was not turned around. Failure to make good on promises of material progress, he said in 1978, was not just an economic matter but "a major political question," one that "exerts a direct influence on the mood and the will to work of the Soviet people." In February 1981 — at the height of Solidarity's power in Poland, a situation surely not far from his mind — he told delegates to the party congress that it was largely on mundane economic matters that the public gauged the party's work. "They judge strictly, exactingly. And this, comrades, we must remember."[28]

When all was said and done, the Brezhnev regime failed to obey its own prescriptions. The General Secretary paid lip service to purging inept officials, smoothly carrying out party resolutions, and remedying the ills of industry and agriculture. In reality, few officials (and none of the eleven ministers lambasted in November 1979) were cashiered, little was done to rescue the innovations and experiments of previous years or to reassess one-time successes gone sour, and no real measures were taken to arrest the economy's deterioration. The exposure of the leadership's promises and ultimatums as hollow demonstrably undermined its credibility.

Brezhnev and his Politburo obviously preferred the costs of inaction to the pain of rethinking their basic approach. Safe, hold-the-line decisions were their chosen path, and they did not deviate from it. In practical, raw power terms, it probably seemed imprudent to tamper — except in speeches — with the implicit post-1964 pledge of semi-permanent job rights for bureaucrats. It was hazardous, also, to promote too many "energetic and creatively thinking comrades," lest they strike out in unwanted ways.

Brezhnevism as a working philosophy was ambiguous from the beginning, combining as it did conservative, reactionary, and reformist tenets. During its final and most stultified phase, the inconsistencies burst into the open, surfacing a fundamental contradiction between policy and the imperatives facing it. By opting for stabilization when imagination was needed, Brezhnev and his cohorts made it far more difficult for those who came after to perpetuate the policies to which they had clung. A leadership that enshrined certainty and stability as its highest values handed its successors uncertainty and, some thought, maybe even potential instability.

2

What Ails the Soviet System?

Contradictions and Difficulties

As the post-Brezhnev era takes shape, the survival of the Soviet system is not in question, but the utility of many of its policies is. The accumulation of internal problems, while leaving the regime well short of all-out crisis, confronts it with choices more vexing than any it has faced in decades. One hallmark of the changing leadership is its sober realism about the extent of these troubles. The former ideological boast that the Soviet Union is a "developed socialist society" has now been replaced by Andropov and Chernenko with the less pretentious claim that the Soviets are still building or "perfecting" developed socialism. The full attainment of socialist ideals, in Andropov's words, "will be a most complicated process, inevitably connected with the overcoming of contradictions and difficulties," certain of which are more intractable than others. "In some areas we will be able to move more quickly, in others more slowly. This is what the real map of social progress is like. It cannot be smoothed out into a straight line."[1]

Some of these "contradictions and difficulties" do not lend themselves to exact measurement. Individual conduct and attitudes at odds with the party's preferences make up one such problem area. The deviations singled out for recent attack by the regime and said to be on the rise in the Soviet Union include abuse of alcohol, crass materialism, corruption, and signs of anomie among the young. Tensions between the Russian majority and the dozens of smaller Soviet nationalities are also difficult to calculate precisely. Andropov, however, found it necessary shortly after being appointed leader to decry "national conceit . . . the tendency toward isolation . . . the disrespectful attitude toward other nations and peoples" finding increasing currency among Soviet ethnic groups.[2]

Other negative trends are more easily pinpointed. Soviet population growth, for example, dropped 50 percent between 1960 and 1980, to 0.8 percent a year. This disturbs a regime inclined to identify national power with population size. It also cramps the growth of the work force, which will expand by only 0.4 percent a year in the 1980s, less than a third of the 1970s' rate and a sixth of the 1960s' figure. And it increases the proportion of retired persons who must be supported by the working population (such people now make up about 16 percent of the total and will be at 20 percent by the year 2000). Perhaps the most unsettling demographic trend is the climb in mortality rates. The Soviet crude death rate, which bottomed out at 6.9 per 1,000 in 1964, jumped by 50 percent to 10.3 in 1980 — a turn of events said by a leading U.S. expert to be "unique in the history of developed countries." The increases posted for infants and men of prime working age were particularly steep.[3]

Easiest to grasp in numerical terms, and of the greatest relevance to politics, are the Soviet Union's economic problems. There is no quibbling over one essential fact: the Soviet economy is in a protracted growth slump, and the population is smarting from the effects. The annual rate of expansion of the Soviet GNP, which topped 5 percent in the early Brezhnev years, dipped to approximately 3 percent in the late 1970s and 2 percent in the early 1980s. Growth in 1983 rebounded to over 3 percent — helped by good weather and Andropov's first economic decisions — but so far most Western specialists are sticking to their overall predictions for the 1980s. It is generally believed that, year-to-year fluctuations aside, the USSR will be fortunate to stay in the vicinity of 2 percent growth for the remainder of the decade.

Economic consumption, measuring the goods and services the Soviet household gets from the economy, is under similar pressure. Growth in per capita consumption slipped to 2.2 percent a year in 1976–80 (as opposed to 5.1 percent ten years before), with food, housing, recreation, and educational and health services faring the worst. It has been projected to rise by only about 1 percent a year in 1981–85 (it actually fell by 1 percent in 1982) and, unless something changes in the meantime, to stagnate completely in the second half of the 1980s. Agriculture, vitally important to the consumer, remains a weak and volatile sector despite massive infusions of resources under Brezhnev. Net agricultural output, which advanced by 3.7 percent a year in 1961–70, was up by an anemic 0.9 percent a year in 1971–79 and was so far below planned levels in 1979–82 that the Soviets withheld production statistics. Though some recovery was evident in 1983, lines outside shops for food and consumer goods are more prevalent than five or ten years ago, local shortages seem more common, and rationing of meat, milk, and other food staples has been reintroduced in some Soviet cities.[4]

Explaining the Soviet Union's Problems

What in the Soviet system explains this piling up of troubles? The underlying difficulties with which today's Politburo and the men who succeed them must grapple can be divided into six categories: the obsolescence of old policy formulas, especially economic ones; the combined challenge of lingering backwardness in key areas and of problems present in a mature industrial society; new doubts about ethnic identity; the widening split between popular expectations and Soviet reality; the turn toward a self-centered morality; and the mixed benefits of the regime's minimal reforms.

Old formulas misfire in new circumstances. As a rule, the Soviet Union addresses its perennial problems with remarkably stable formulas and approaches. It lives by time-tested practice. The catch is that sooner or later all old habits generate diminishing returns. This waning effectiveness of inherited solutions accounts for much of the load under which the regime now labors.

Old formulas often lose their efficacy because the conditions under which they were first worked out evolve more quickly than the formula itself. In the Soviet case, there are any number of illustrations. For instance, the Soviet indoctrination network, set up after the Revolution to carry the party's gospel to an illiterate or semi-literate population, has far less impact on today's more sophisticated public. A hospital and clinic system that did well at introducing elementary health care and curbing epidemic disease in a largely agrarian country is less in step with an urbanized and industrialized society with high stress levels, heavy pollution, richer diets, and greater alcohol consumption.

This pattern of declining returns bears particularly upon the Soviet economy. In Charles Lindblom's apt characterization, the traditional Soviet economic model is "strong thumbs, no fingers."[5] State ownership, central planning, direct administrative control over factories and farms, and periodic campaigns for implementing the latest priorities are its main features. For several decades after being put into operation in Stalin's early five-year plans, the powerful thumbs of the command economy did give rise to a quite acceptable pace of growth. After a certain point, however, they have proven to be maladroit. Not only has Soviet economic growth ebbed, it has also lagged significantly in relation to other industrial economies. One comparison shows Soviet growth, which had outstripped sixteen OECD countries by 0.4 percent a year in 1966–70, to have fallen 1 percent behind in the late 1970s. In terms of per capita consumption, the Soviet Union trailed OECD annual growth by 1.4 percent, reversing an earlier Soviet advantage of 0.6 percent. After making some headway in closing the chasm between Soviet and Western standards of living, the Soviets have seen it open up again since the mid-1970s, especially in housing, recreation, health and education.[6]

Finer, suppler fingers of economic management are needed today because circumstances have changed: the cheap resources around which the original Soviet blueprint for industrialization was drawn up have been largely exhausted. The effect of the coarse thumbs of the classic formula was, to use the terminology of economic analysis (Soviet as well as Western), "extensive" in nature, pressing into service as speedily as possible the Soviet Union's abundance of labor, capital, land, energy, and raw materials. Now, continued development requires an "intensive" strategy, oriented toward the more effective use of scarce resources, with better incentives, coordination, and technological innovation. On all these scores, Soviet achievements have been unimpressive. Total factor productivity in the Soviet economy (the increase in output per added unit of capital and labor input) is the best global measure of this. After rising by 1.5 percent in the 1960s, it inched up by 0.1 percent a year in the first half of the 1970s, then *decreased* by an annual average of 0.4 percent in the second half of the 1970s, and of about 1 percent in 1981–82.[7]

Policies are often questioned and revised when their architects pass from the scene. In the Soviet Union, many policy canons devised in the regime's formative years have endured. They have in a sense been written into the operating codes of the huge state and party bureaucracies running the country. In this situation, there is a tendency for the administrative apparatus, untroubled by the discipline of the market or by direct accountability to society, to act as "a gigantic machine that slowly and inflexibly grinds along in the direction in which it was initially aimed."[8] In principle, Soviet politicians are no less free than any others to attack and redirect the bureaucracy beneath them. In practice, they have done so only in fits and starts — and were especially loath to do so very much during the long Brezhnev era.

The problems of success meet the problems of backwardness. Besides perennial problems such as assuring steady industrial growth, for which old formulas yield shrinking dividends, political problems of two different sorts have cropped up in the Soviet Union. First, as the leaders have known for some time, the very accomplishments of the country in building an industrial economy and a modern, urban society have been bringing it up against the new and unanticipated worries of success. "Life goes forward," Brezhnev said as early as 1967. Once the regime's main challenges had been vanquishing internal enemies and laying an industrial base, but now "new tasks stand before us, new not only in scale but in character."[9]

Many of the emergent problems of maturity are less economic and technical than social and cultural. Thus environmental pollution, a by-product of unregulated industrialization long passed over by the government, became in the 1960s and 1970s an important issue for widening portions of the Soviet population, and it is bound to remain so. In big Soviet cities, traffic congestion, in its own way a proof of economic advancement, poses a serious concern. In the cities, too, the profusion of huge tracts of high-rise housing, welcomed by all as a needed response to the apartment shortage, has created a faceless and monotonous milieu. Soviet discussions of what to do about it remind one of inquiries in other developed countries.[10] In natural science, Soviet breakthroughs in molecular biology and recombinant DNA research have raised the same issues of technique and conscience found abroad. The foreign reader of Soviet debates on genetic engineering "is increasingly struck by the similarity of these discussions to the ones that have been occurring in the West."[11]

What is fascinating about the Soviet Union today is the simultaneous eruption of these problems associated with progress and of a second set of problems usually linked with economic and social backwardness. Difficulties the regime thought it had resolved, or at least held in check, have in recent years come back to haunt it. This re-animation of dormant problems has multiple causes: exceptionally clumsy or ossified policies, the reduced allocation of resources, and bills coming due for what might be called deferred social maintenance — all accentuated as short-term gains are traded for long-term effectiveness.

Examples abound. The bulge in death rates points to a regression in the health care system, and perhaps in the quality of Soviet life more broadly. Since 1969 the completion of new apartments has failed to keep up with the number of new families, thanks to the housing lobby's poor showing in the budget wars after Khrushchev's fall. Soviet urbanologists, who for some time had turned their pens to more complicated and subtle matters such as the esthetics of mass housing and the impersonality of city life, have begun to write again about the quantitative shortage of housing with a plaintiveness not heard since the 1950s. Some Western experts think that the Soviet farm system entered a period of absolute decline in the 1970s. Certain of the regime's own actions lend credence to such a conclusion, notably its decision in early 1979 — before the latest string of bad harvests — to make mandatory what had been a spontaneous move toward re-establishing subsidiary plots and gardens at industrial plants and other non-farm enterprises.[12] Most of these woefully inadequate facilities had been phased out decades before. For the average Russian, once again seeing a cabbage patch or chicken coop in the courtyard of his factory or institute is a throwback to the lean 1930s and wartime years and a sad commentary on the collective and state farms. Some take it as an omen of worse times ahead.

New questions about ethnic identity. Roots of the regime's difficulties are also found in the multinational composition of Soviet society. The 137 million Russians, though far and away the largest single group, constituted a bare majority (52 percent) of the Soviet population in the latest, 1979 census. A hundred-odd nationalities, living under Moscow's sway since before the Revolution though still concentrated in their ancestral territories, are arrayed in a great arc around the Russian heartland. The Russians' fellow Slavs (Ukrainians and Belorussians) account for 20 percent of the population, with the other major European groups representing 8 percent. Of the remainder, the biggest bloc by far is the 17 percent of Moslem heritage, based mostly in Central Asia, Kazakhstan, and the Transcaucasus. Among the twenty-one non-Russian nationalities numbering more than a million, the majority of the members of all but two speak mainly their mother tongue.

The temperature of Soviet ethnic politics has heated up perceptibly in the last ten or fifteen years. In Khrushchev's day, the regime spoke optimistically of eliminating ethnic divisions and eventually assimilating the smaller peoples into the Russian majority. Now the Soviet view is far less rosy, placing emphasis on the stubbornness of ethnic identities and the hazards of ethnic conflict. In the most straightforward acknowledgment of the problem to date, Yuri Andropov declared in December 1982 that the economic and social development of ethnic communities "is inevitably accompanied by the growth of their national self-consciousness," not by its decline. The ideal of fusing the Soviet nationalities into one has not been discarded, but it has been relegated to the remote future, after a classless and fully communist society has been constructed. In the meantime, Andropov said, "problems in the relations among nationalities will not be crossed off our agenda. They demand the special concern and constant attention of the Communist Party."[13]

The symptoms of Soviet ethnic dissension are several. First, as Andropov's remarks attest, the regime itself now takes the problem more seriously than in the past. It has accepted the need for what he labeled "a well thought-out, scientifically based nationality policy," and to this end has sponsored frank empirical research on nationality questions and solicited advice from experts in the field.[14]

Second, there has been an acceleration of protest over issues of nationality, spearheaded by members of the emerging middle classes of the non-Russian groups. Ethnic grievances have become a major theme in political dissent in non-Russian areas, and charges have been levelled against local politicians for sympathizing (Pyotr Shelest, the head of the large Ukrainian branch of the party, for example, was dismissed and indicted as a closet Ukrainian nationalist in 1972). There have also been mass public demonstrations against Moscow's cultural and linguistic policy in several areas, notably in Lithuania in 1972 (where paratroopers had to be called in to suppress the crowds) and in Georgia during the discussion of the republic's constitution in 1978. Strange though it may sound, even the Great Russians, or at least many intellectuals among them, are feeling a similar frustration and pent-up nationalism. Like Lithuanians, Georgians, or Uzbeks, "they too are concerned about the right to express their national identity [and] about the homogenization of their culture."[15]

Third, ethnic emotions seem to intrude increasingly into the economic and socioeconomic spheres. This is true in the competition for investment resources, which has become keener as Soviet economic growth has subsided. Partisans of big regional projects—like exploitation of Siberian oil and gas, rerouting of northern rivers to parched Central Asia, and rehabilitation of the Ukraine's Donbass coal fields—have invoked national pride and rights along with narrowly economic arguments. Similarly, rivalry between Russians and non-Russians over professional and administrative jobs has picked up in the minority areas, despite an "affirmative action" policy favoring native personnel for most positions. Crackdowns on local corruption rings have also sparked ethnic controversy, producing "false lamentations that merciless criticism of negative phenomena somehow infringes upon national honor."[16]

Finally, a long shadow is cast over the future of Soviet ethnic relations by demographic trends. The most alarming from the Russian vantage point is the enormous asymmetry in fertility between the European population and the other Soviet peoples. The rate of births per 1,000 population is now two and a half times greater in Central Asia, where large families are favored by culture and climate, than in the Slavic republics, where one child is the average couple's aim. Whereas the Russian population will creep up by 2.4 million between 1979 and 2000, the Moslem total is expected to grow by 20 million. By the turn of the century, the Russians, with 47 percent of the population and only about 40 percent of all 0-to-9-year-olds, will no longer be a majority.[17]

The growing expectations gap.   Never is there a perfect match between what a government does and what its public expects it to do. What count politically are the size of the gap and the direction in which it is moving. One element in the Soviet regime's present predicament is that a large and widening gulf has opened between performance and aspirations.

To the ultrarepressive Stalinist state of a generation ago, Soviet citizens did look for some minimal benefits, as interviews with refugees at the time established. From this low starting point, popular aspirations escalated rapidly in the wake of Stalin's death. The regime's own rhetorical excesses were partly responsible for this—the bragging of the Communist Party Program of 1961 that Soviet prosperity would eclipse the United States' by 1980 being perhaps the most hyperbolic such promise. (As it happened, Soviet GNP per capita was only one-third of the American in 1980.) Of more consequence was the tacit but clear pact with society that, with the shedding of both indiscriminate political terror and social utopianism, the regime was henceforth to be judged essentially by its ability to "deliver the goods" to the people.[18] Though the Brezhnev leadership muffled the Khrushchevian sloganeering, it left the basic vow intact.

Mass aspirations have also been aroused by the rising educational profile of the population, which has stimulated young people to desire respected and rewarding careers in which their knowledge can be used. Another accelerator has been the unlimbering of communication within Soviet society, both among professionals and at the level of the mass media—especially television, which came into general use only under Brezhnev. This has spotlighted the regime's specific failings and contributed to a broadly based yearning for the good things of life.[19] Enriched contact with the outside world has also played a role. Here, even more effective than awareness of the West's wealth has been the example of the communist states of Eastern Europe, to which Soviet citizens have had far greater exposure and where Soviet-like institutions generally serve consumers better than in the USSR.

The regime's performance since Stalin in meeting mass expectations has been satisfactory in a fundamental sense. But it is also true that the regime has been losing ground: the distance between its actions and society's aspirations is now increasing. On many issues, including consumer goods and food, the slide is associated with the later phases of Brezhnevism. On others, it began somewhat earlier.

Possibly, some in the regime console themselves with the notion that poor performance by Soviet institutions has sometimes acted to depress expectations. Consider one question well studied by Soviet sociologists: diminishing access by ambitious Soviet youth to high-status occupations. If in the early 1960s 57 percent of all secondary-school graduates were being admitted to higher education, the stepping-stone to a professional career, by a decade later (as many more tenth-graders jostled for entrance) only 22 percent were making it in.[20] Following their initial disappointment, many young people in fact adapted to the new conditions by entering technical and vocational programs and lowering their sights. Once in the work force, they often "feel themselves in social terms to be no worse off than those who became [university] students and acquired a diploma. . . . Youth is quite tactfully grasping the change in the real situation."[21]

This, however, does not mean the larger problem is self-correcting. For one thing, expectations thwarted in some areas are being diverted into others. As one sociologist wrote in 1975 about the young person barred entrance to the university, such an individual tends to seek out satisfactions "that would compensate for his loss," including higher pay and better leisure.[22] Nor do expectations seem to be ebbing nearly as quickly as regime performance. Studies of Soviet buying habits observe that consumers now feel entitled to more and better goods than in the past, that "the demands of people have significantly grown, and industry trails along behind them."[23] Over the whole gamut of issues, particularly those touching on consumer welfare, it is fair to say that the expectations gap has been stretched out during the last decade.

Another telling fact about expectations is that under Soviet conditions the continued wilting among the population of hope and belief in the future is apt to be extremely damaging to the regime itself. In a system where the state is simultaneously employer and provider of goods and services, popular pessimism can feed back directly onto the state's ability to realize its own goals. While some puncturing of unrealistic expectations has been expedient, past a certain juncture it becomes counterproductive because it undermines people's willingness to work. There are many in the Soviet Union who think that this divide has already been reached, that disaffected workers and managers are simply putting out less on the job. This "social factor," as it is often referred to, is the final link in a vicious circle: society gets and expects less, so it gives less; the state promises and gives less, so it gets less. One Soviet economist, correctly I think, has placed the expectations gap and the motivation issue at the hub of the regime's present dilemma. Inducing the worker-consumer to produce in a low-growth economy with a flat earnings structure "now forms a unique 'solar plexus,' the center of all the socioeconomic problems of our society."[24]

The reach for private solutions. Because of the regime's faltering capacity to satisfy popular demands, Soviet citizens increasingly seek gratification from other sources. This interest did not originate in the last ten or fifteen years, but it clearly gathered momentum during that time. The partial withdrawal of citizens from public life takes an array of forms, compounding the Soviet system's many other difficulties.

Greater independence and self-centeredness are a badge of most Soviet political dissent, including the movement for Jewish emigration. They have also become a compelling force in culture and the arts. The most noticeable feature of Soviet literature, once devoted to preaching the virtues of collectivism, is now "its preoccupation with private human concerns."[25] Recent novels and poetry dwell on individual melancholy, fatigue, and solitude.

Ordinary folk exhibit the same spirit when, the blandishments of the regime to the contrary, they follow their own lights in making the key life-cycle decisions. Divorces, abortions, and illegitimate births, all legal but frowned upon, are more numerous. In the European regions, women have fewer children than the government wants, in Asia more. Choices about employment and location are weakly regulated and costly to Moscow's plans, all owing to "the fact that migration depends on the personal element, on the taking by the individual of the voluntary decision to change his place of residence."[26] Escape of a different nature is provided by vodka, the consumption of which climbs at tempos disconcerting to the leaders, the medical profession, and many others. Soviet per capita consumption of alcoholic beverages, rated in liters of pure alcohol, rose 50 percent between 1965 and 1979, one of the highest rates of increase anywhere; purchases of state-produced alcohol (not counting moonshine) soak up 15 percent of total disposable income.[27]

Individualism thrives particularly in the Soviet economy. Since cash incomes outrun the supply of desired goods and services and the prices of most essential commodities are frozen, Soviet consumers have taken to withholding unprecedented amounts of money from circulation. Bank and other savings in 1976 were equivalent to two-thirds of the population's money income and 84 percent of retail sales that year.[28] This bloated reserve of currency is a lien on future production, a reminder of popular disenchantment, and a disincentive to hard work. Hoarding of scarce commodities has also become more widespread, especially after the mid-1970s. The upshot is artificial shortages and the feeding of black markets.[29]

"Colored markets" of every tint — black, grey, pink, and others recognized in the argot of the street — have swelled in the Soviet Union, testimony to the inability of official structures to accommodate individual ingenuity. As one Soviet discussion puts it, "The person is not at all a bolt that can be snapped into a machine and forced to work there. He does not simply adjust to the system of economic relations. He also actively studies it, finds if necessary its weak spots, and tries wherever possible to use them."[30] In Soviet industry and agriculture, there is more barter outside the plan, resulting often in what the Soviets term "protectionism," or networks for exchanging nonpecuniary favors. Bumping up against the low ceiling on earnings set by wage egalitarianism, more of the able and restless members of society shunt their efforts into the illegal "second economy," as Western analysts now call it. Frustrated consumers buy more of what they need *nalevo* (on the side) from friends, freelancing producers and middlemen, sales clerks, waiters, and so on. Choice goods are either stolen from store shelves or manufactured from scratch by underground entrepreneurs. They find ready buyers at inflated prices because, by Andropov's admission, state production is often so bad "that people prefer to overpay the speculator for articles that are good and made with taste."[31]

Dishonesty among Soviet officials has also been on the ascent, as numerous official and unofficial sources tell us. The economic slowdown and the unremitting pressure to fulfill production quotas have spawned more false and padded reporting (*pripiska*) by managers. This in turn has a demoralizing effect on the work force as a whole. "Where there is lack of correspondence between the visible, real results of production and the announced results, such as is completely obvious to the collective, this dispirits workers . . . negatively affects the attitude toward socialist property . . . stimulates the erosion of moral values."[32]

Most menacing to the regime has been the heightened incidence of outright corruption. As of Brezhnev's death, neither regional purges nor repeated editorial scoldings had made large inroads into it. Admonitions to officials feathering their nests became especially piquant in the early 1980s, some hinting that malefactors were finding protection from the police and from political bigwigs. "The use of state and public property and official position for the purpose of personal enrichment" was a major motif in Yuri Andropov's early pronouncements as party leader. The policeman or bureaucrat on the take, he stated on one occasion, is striking "nothing less than a blow at the very essence of our system."[33]

The mixed blessings of minimal reforms.   A final cause of the present Soviet malady lies in the regime's preferred way of coping with its problems. The minimal reforms typical of the Brezhnev era, diffident and unhurried as they were, have worked on balance to the benefit of the regime and the population. But they have also engendered costs and frictions that new leaders will be obliged to come to terms with one way or another.

Again it is the economy that drives the point home. Here the skin-deep revision of structures and operating rules since the mid-1960s has been much less disruptive than the spasmodic renovations of the Khrushchev years. Yet, tinkering changes, followed by measures to fine-tune what were from the start inadequate measures, are "becoming a part of the problem, rather than contributing to its solution."[34] Under Brezhnev, the leadership frequently resorted to local experiments, launched in one sector or place and then slowly extended elsewhere. While the pragmatic and consultative manner in which the pilot projects were formulated and executed was often preferred to past ways, the aggregate effect has been to complicate the administration of the economy without drastically improving it. The experiments have siphoned time and energy off into monitoring, reporting, and analysis. Most of them, after many dry runs, have not been comprehensively introduced. When expensive equipment has been imported to assist in local innovation, it limps along at a fraction of its potential because the Soviets have not provided the necessary supports. Computers—hooked up without the proper software, telecommunications, and maintenance facilities—are the most conspicuous case.[35]

Irresolute reforms have been most in evidence when it comes to consumer welfare. Agriculture excepted, the regime has attempted to satisfy popular demands for housing, soft and durable goods, and personal services without reallocating budgetary resources in any emphatic way. It has also shrunk from creating potent new organizations able to do the job on their own. Instead, institutions with different missions entirely are ordered to add consumer-directed tasks to their existing repertoires. Industrial construction firms are obliged to build housing, truck factories and radar plants produce refrigerators and televisions, and in some remote towns industrial enterprises operate bus and streetcar lines. Established organizations do these things with neither enthusiasm nor efficiency. Hence consumer programs are poorly funded, weakly coordinated, and the first to be harmed when something goes awry.

The production of consumer goods for private purchase, a sore point made more tender in the late Brezhnev years, is a good illustration. Soviet light industry plants, which manufacture mostly for the mass market, still find themselves at the end of the supply queue. The resultant slack in production is taken up by heavy industry, which makes half of all non-food goods, including all vehicles and most home appliances. In spite of years of exhortation, heavy industry executives generally have "the attitude that the production of articles for the consumer is something of secondary importance."[36] Subject to little direction from above, they produce a jumble of models that are designed within individual plants, mutually incompatible, and frequently out of touch with consumer needs and tastes. They thus inflict upon the Soviet household no fewer than 130 refrigerator models (most of them outdated), 70 kinds of vacuum cleaners, 56 different television sets, 50 table radios, 40 sewing machines, and 34 electric razors. With the manufacturer accepting next to no responsibility for spare parts or servicing, the consumer is left to fend for himself if, as often happens, something goes wrong with his purchase.

A uniquely perverse outcome has developed in the field of low-priced household goods, known in Soviet parlance as "goods of the simplest selection, not centrally planned." For about 85 percent of these approximately 3,000 items, central control consists solely of assigning global quotas, expressed in rubles and not in physical units, to the industrial ministries, which are then given carte blanche to decide what to make and distribute. "No one," a retailing official grumbled in 1982, "is occupied with coordinating the production of the whole range of the simplest commodities, and in this lies the source of many omissions and failures."[37] Salt has been rubbed in this old wound since the mid-1970s as plant managers, pressed to meet their basic plans, cut back arbitrarily on the manufacture of household goods. Faced with targets reckoned in gross ruble terms, they have often opted for shorter runs of larger, costlier items and produced fewer of the cheaper but often more necessary articles.[38] This explains the recent proliferation of shortages of such inexpensive but irreplaceable consumer goods as paper products (of which there is a permanent shortage), tooth brushes, underwear and lingerie, baby blankets and diapers, low-wattage light bulbs, ink, glue, small bottles, aspirin, bandages, light footwear, needles and thread, inexpensive radios, kitchen utensils, ironing boards, axes, spades, garden hoses, wooden stools, key rings, hinges, bolts, shoe polish, electric switches, spark plugs, piston rings, typewriter ribbons, bath soap, and washing machine detergent.

Minimal reforms with this result may be worse than no change at all. An individual might, after all, be philosophical about not owning a washing machine; when the machine he does own cannot be repaired or stands idle for lack of detergent, he is apt to be less forgiving. Such experiences beget popular disillusionment, fuel the underground economy, and prod demands for more fundamental revisions of policy.

The Danger of Crisis

What can be concluded about the Soviet Union's problems and their underlying causes? Some in the West suggest the USSR today is a society in crisis, that it has come to a turning point in which the very continuance of the Soviet order is at stake. The thesis is wrong. It understates the rulers' resources and overstates their problems.

In surveying the Soviet regime's worries, one must not lose sight of its strengths and assets. The Soviet system is now in its seventh decade. Having weathered more than its fair share of trials and shocks—civil strife, forced-draft industrialization, the great purges, a devastating war with 20 million casualties, de-Stalinization, and the overthrow of Khrushchev—its resilience can hardly be doubted. Its stability is based in large part on sturdy instruments of control—the single-party system, the political police and armed forces, censorship, denial of free assembly, comprehensive political education, and the like—none of which shows signs of cracking. The telltale mark of a political system in mortal danger is violence, and political violence has been kept to a singularly low level in the Soviet Union. There have been impromptu strikes, the occasional street demonstration, and scattered acts of terrorism; but little blood has been spilled, and the authorities have with relative ease limited the fallout from such incidents.

Among the forces aligned against the regime, there is barely a soul who either advocates its forcible overthrow or sees any realistic chance of this happening.

The regime's solidity rests also on a record of positive achievements. Whatever its shortcomings, it has made the country a world military power, safe for the first time from foreign invasion. At great sacrifice, its economic programs and science have ferried peasant Russia into the space age. Economic development and free public schooling have drawn millions of Soviets from humble backgrounds into attractive professional and administrative careers. Cradle-to-grave social services and safeguards, expanded under Brezhnev for the peasantry, give Soviet citizens a security few would happily surrender (and that most emigrants from the USSR seem to miss dearly). All told, the regime's accomplishments represent a store of political capital on which it can draw for some time. Recent Soviet failures, it must be remembered, have in the main been failures at the margin. Many would not have happened but for previous successes. Economic growth has slowed down, but the economy has not ceased to grow, let alone given indications of breaking down. There is a shortage of steak but not of bread, of blue jeans but not of work boots, of living space but not of basic shelter.

Granted that it has been jarred by recent events, basic support for Soviet institutions has thus far not really been loosened. As one thoughtful observer puts it, "there is no evidence that [the] perceived legitimacy of the system has lessened . . . among any but the relatively small contingent of dissidents and critically minded intellectuals." Though there has been a welling up of pessimism, especially in the middle class, there is still a residue of optimism about the future, "a feeling that in the very long run things will turn out all right." Present discontent is directed at the performance of the Soviet system and not its existence.[39]

Before being carried away with the trouble the Soviets are in, it is also useful to compare their difficulties with those of other countries. It may be overdoing it to say, as does one American commentator, that talk of declining growth and structural problems in the Soviet economy "could describe any country in the world."[40] Still, it is all too tempting in reciting the litany of Soviet woes to forget the recent Western recession, that cash wages in the United States (adjusted for inflation) are below what they were ten years ago, and that there are more than 25 million men and women out of work in Western Europe and North America. The Politburo's headaches do not include, as those of the cabinets of the liberal democracies have lately, sky-high budget deficits, key industries ravaged by foreign competition, race riots, or separatist movements. Making due allowance for its deficiencies, the USSR still possesses the second largest economy in the world, leading all other countries in the production of steel, cement, and many types of machinery. With enormous reserves of natural gas, oil, coal, and hydropower, it has by far the most favorable long-term energy balance of any industrial power.

None of this is to make light of Soviet problems. They are real, they are worsening, and they are having a cumulative effect. While the Soviet system has not arrived at the point of crisis, it clearly is headed in the wrong direction, raising the specter of grave trouble down the road. Some Soviet leaders have guardedly conceded as much. Writing in the party's theoretical journal in 1981, Konstantin Chernenko, then Brezhnev's closest ally in the leadership, enjoined the party to recognize anew the importance of serving "the proper interests" of all segments of society. With Poland obviously in mind, he warned that otherwise, "our policy risks losing its firm social base, its support on the part of the masses." Poor analysis of social problems and disregard of the interests of particular classes and groups are, he said, "fraught with *the danger of social tension, of political and socioeconomic crisis.*"[41] Andropov several times struck a similar chord during his brief leadership. "It is necessary to pay dearly for one's mistakes in politics," he told the Central Committee in June 1983. "If the party's bond with the people is lost, into the resultant vacuum come self-styled pretenders to the role of spokesman for the interests of the working people"—a pointed allusion to Lech Walesa and the Solidarity union.[42]

Which problems are most capable of shearing "the party's bond with the people"? Which will command priority attention because they have the potential of realizing the admitted danger of a general crisis of the Soviet system? For a problem to be critical in this sense, it must satisfy two criteria. First, it must be severe enough to affect the essential well-being of society and the cooperative relations among its members. Second, it must be urgent, calling for prompt action, as distinct from a condition that is stable or that worsens only slowly.

Some of the problems on the Soviet agenda, while far from trivial, fail to qualify as critical by the touchstone of severity. Genetic engineering, pollution, traffic tie-ups, and city planning will agitate many officials and citizens in the years to come, yet they are not likely to be a great burden to the top leaders. They may act as a drain on resources needed to resolve more basic problems (as, say, concern over pollution does in relation to some kinds of industrial growth), but they are not of sufficient weight to alter the leadership's core agenda. The problems of health care, bad as they may be, are also non-critical from a political perspective. They have provoked little reaction outside a restricted circle of administrators and experts, and there is evidence that the Soviets managed in the middle and late 1970s to reverse the downward trend in at least one major field (infant mortality).[43] Answers in this instance are probably a simple matter of resources. There can be little question that Soviet health standards can resume their historic upward movement, provided that the necessary allocations are made to treatment, research, and prophylaxis.

Still other Soviet problems do not meet the test of urgency. This is true of demographic issues. What Soviet leader in the 1980s is going to lose sleep over family-planning decisions that will not be reflected in manpower levels until after the turn of the century, long after he is out of power? The same holds for the reduction in opportunities for Soviet youth to enter desirable careers. Once any society has passed through the early stages of industrialization and the most prized occupational slots have been filled (and the children of the winners given a head start in competing for plum positions in the next generation), it is difficult if not impossible to retain the high rates of upward mobility realized at the outset. For the individuals involved, the problem may be severe; for the government, it cannot be urgent, for there is no tangible remedy short of upending other policies (such as job security for qualified incumbents).

The Soviet Union's problem of ethnic relations is often discussed by foreign observers in apocalyptic language, sometimes as if the Soviet multinational state were on the verge of collapsing like a house of cards. But careful reflection suggests it, too, is not a critically urgent problem. The Soviet regime has in the past been extraordinarily adept at using sticks and carrots to keep the non-Russian minorities in line. Two or three generations into the future, population dynamics alone may make fundamental change inescapable. Over the next ten years or so, however, and even several decades beyond, the problem seems readily manageable.

Russian hegemony in its present form is in no serious peril for several reasons. First, demographic trends, distressing though they may be to the Russians, will leave them and their Slavic cousins in an ascendant numerical position long into the twenty-first century. Russians, Ukrainians, and Belorussians will comprise 65 percent of the USSR's population in 2000, three times the Moslem proportion. Second, political leverage will not automatically spring from demographic growth. Political power is an independent Russian resource, and they will use it to ensure that as much of it as possible is passed on to future Russians. Third, the dominant Russians will go on enjoying the advantage of territorial and political coherence and priority. The ethnic minorities will remain on the periphery, penetrated by large Russian settler communities (24 million Russians lived in the non-Russian republics in 1979, making up almost a fifth of the population there), relatively isolated from one another, and able in most cases to communicate with one another only in Russian. Fourth, Russian tolerance of native traditions, successful economic modernization, and other factors should keep the region that poses the greatest demographic challenge—

Central Asia—long receptive to Soviet rule. The vast majority of Soviet Central Asians seem content with the regime and would find the arguments of an Ayatollah Khomeini, which have wreaked such havoc across the Iranian border, "very difficult . . . to understand, let alone endorse."[44] Fifth, Moscow will have the opportunity of building on the one great success of nationality policy under Brezhnev: Russian-language training. Between 1970 and 1979, the proportion of non-Russians knowing Russian as a first or second language rose from 49 to 62 percent; the ratio is much higher among urban residents and younger people. An intensified teaching program unveiled in the late 1970s and affirmed in May 1983 by Andropov's Politburo should keep the trend in train.[45]

There is, however, an item on the Soviet agenda that is sufficiently severe and urgent to be truly critical, one that could lead to a general crisis of the regime. That is the problem to which this chapter has repeatedly turned for examples—the problem of the economy. For the Soviet Union, the central question of the coming decade is that of its sputtering economic engine and of the social ramifications of economic stagnation.

Economic difficulties are by far the most common precipitant of political trauma and change. In well-nigh all industrial societies today, economic and socioeconomic issues dominate political debate. The Soviet Union is no different: elite and mass opinion alike take it as a given that economic and related problems are and will continue to be of overriding importance. The regime's rhetoric, programs, and anxieties all revolve around the economy. The population, for its part, sizes up the state today more than ever by how it delivers the goods in industry and agriculture.

Moreover, the health of the economy has a direct bearing on many of the non-economic issues facing the Soviet system. Prized foreign policy goals are implicated, since high military expenditures and international prestige are harder to sustain in a sluggish economy. At home, almost all major interests would be poorly served by continuing economic malaise. Soviet communists have been no less inclined than American liberals to see economic growth as a surrogate for painful, redistributive choice among competing priorities. The worse the economy does, the more those conflicts—guns versus butter, schools versus hospitals, the holders of jobs versus the aspirants to jobs—have to be sorted out and defused. The more also ethnic harmony will be injured, for retarded growth in an unreformed Soviet economy would exacerbate the competition for investment funds that pits region against region. Ethnic and regional imbalances in labor supply add to the problem. The entire increment to the Soviet work force in the 1980s will occur in the Moslem areas, whereas the number of persons employed in the built-up Russian and Ukrainian republics will actually decline. Unless economic productivity and growth prospects are improved in the established European regions, the regime will face two options either of which is likely to inflame ethnic relations: involuntary importation of millions of Central Asian workers into the Slavic republics, which could both anger the Central Asians and create ethnic ghettos in Slavic cities; or, equally unpalatable, redirection of new investment and maybe even existing industrial plant into the Moslem regions.

It is on economic and socioeconomic issues that the gap between regime performance and popular expectations has grown most dangerously in recent years. To make matters worse, it is here that the Soviets seem now to be the victims of several vicious circles, that is to say, of negative economic trends that feed on themselves. Two of these have already been mentioned: the contribution of inadequate rewards to poor work motivation and, therefore, to low productivity, which in turn reduces the total available for rewards; and the substitution of private for public responses to economic needs, spinning off worlds of activity not under the regime's direct control and in conflict with its values. A third vicious circle involves economic investment, which is now desperately needed to replace aging capital stock in manufacturing and transport and to bring on stream new sources of energy and raw materials, many of them in locations remote from the thickly populated European territory. Although by world standards Soviet investment is high (over 30 percent of GNP), its rate of growth was halved after 1975 (from 7.0 percent a year in 1971–75 to 3.5 percent in 1976–80) and is set at a sickly 1 percent a year for the planning period 1981–85. Force-fed with capital for half a century, the Soviet economy is now being put on starvation rations because the economic growth that sustains the production of capital goods is wavering and because, in circumstances of declining growth, the political leadership was unwilling to rank investment ahead of maintaining levels of mass consumption and military spending. To many Soviet and Western experts, this decision, absent any compensating measures, makes official growth projections more a wish list than a firm plan and heavily mortgages future recovery.[46]

There can be no grounds whatever for the Kremlin hoping that the present economic crunch will prove to be transitory and that developments a few years hence will ring in a period of new and easy prosperity. Most speculation to this effect, in the Soviet Union and abroad, has turned on the question of manpower supply. Even if more cheap workers could bail the economy out of its difficulties (a dubious proposition), the latest Soviet predictions, done after the 1979 census, show no relief in sight. The supply of new labor will improve briefly after 1990, only to worsen quickly after 1995. Net additions to the working-age population in the 1990s as a whole will be 1 million persons fewer than in the stringent 1980s and almost 17 million fewer than in the relatively benign 1970s.[47]

To sum up: the agenda of Soviet politics is indeed a disquieting one. Dwindling payoffs to old solutions, the combination of the novel problems of success and the resurgent problems of neglect, the accentuation of ethnic tensions, the inability of the regime to meet rising expectations, the spread of self-seeking behavior in such forms as corruption and the second economy, the failures of fainthearted reforms — all are harbingers of more trouble ahead. The Soviet system is not yet in crisis, but unless its new leaders can brake downward trends, especially in the economy, the time may not be very far off when it will be.

3
The Changing Soviet Elite

The Andropov Interlude

The Soviet leadership in the Brezhnev era was as unchanging as the policy it fostered. That ended with a jolt at the start of the 1980s. In short order, Aleksei Kosygin, Mikhail Suslov, and Brezhnev died and Andrei Kirilenko was set aside, decimating the inner core of the Politburo that had dominated Soviet politics since Khrushchev's ouster twenty years ago. What course the Soviet Union will now take depends in the first instance on the leaders to come, and above all on the primary leader. The party General Secretary, even in a collective leadership, is uniquely situated to steer decisions. The competition over his office is one of the dramas of Soviet politics and historically has been a prime catalyst of change. The protracted struggle to succeed Brezhnev has already generated significant innovation in policy and is likely to continue doing so as it proceeds. Andropov, the victor in the first heat, brought a new approach to the Kremlin and, with it, promises of controlled reform. He made a rapid start on consolidating his power and delivering on his promises, but just as rapidly he succumbed to health problems and died with his changes in an embryonic state.

Yuri Vladimirovich Andropov came to office a hard-nosed and resourceful politician with lengthy and varied service to the party cause. Born in a Russian railway clerk's family in 1914, a party member since 1939, and the graduate of a vocational institute for water transport personnel, he held a string of provincial posts in the youth league and party apparatus before working in the Central Committee's cadres department in the final two years of Stalin's life. He was transferred in 1953 to foreign policy, serving first as ambassador to Hungary and then as department head and secretary in the central party apparatus responsible for liaison with other communist countries. In May 1967 Brezhnev made him chief of the KGB, in which capacity he was co-opted to candidate Politburo membership in

1967 and to full membership in April 1973. In May 1982, following Suslov's death, Andropov again became a national party secretary, this time answering broadly for ideology and foreign policy.

Andropov's assumption of power paralleled previous successions in several respects. Brezhnev, like all Soviet leaders before him, had not managed and probably had not wished to designate an heir. As before, the institutional hierarchy determined the crucial decision, with the Politburo choosing Andropov and the larger Central Committee merely ratifying the choice. As in the past, the winner came from among the tiny number of politicians sitting on both the Politburo and the Secretariat, the nerve center of the party's administrative apparatus. Besides Andropov, only three others held dual Politburo-Secretariat office upon Brezhnev's death in November 1982: Brezhnev's former personal retainer, Konstantin Chernenko, the senior secretary responsible for cadres selection and by all accounts Brezhnev's preferred successor; Mikhail Gorbachev, the newest and youngest face in the leadership and its specialist on agriculture and the consumer industry; and Kirilenko, once Brezhnev's heir-apparent but by this time ill and in such bad political odor that he had been informally dropped from the Politburo lineup. With Kirilenko out of the running and Gorbachev hampered by his relative youth and inexperience, the issue boiled down to Andropov versus Chernenko. Here, as in previous successions, clandestine infighting and alliance building, initiated months before the outgoing leader's departure, played their part. The outcome was decided by some combination of Andropov's adroitness at intrigue and capacity for leadership and Chernenko's handicaps, chiefly his lack of independent stature.

In certain other ways, Andropov's ascent deviated from precedent. It was conspicuous for its efficiency, for the lack of visible policy quarrels accompanying it, and for the fact that for the first time since the 1920s the old leader was not openly repudiated. Andropov also was atypical in the speed with which he gathered the reins of formal power into his hands. Six months after becoming General Secretary, he was publicly identified as Chairman of the Defense Council, the supreme decision organ for national security; the following month, on June 16, 1983, he was named Chairman of the Presidium of the Supreme Soviet, or head of state. Brezhnev got these appointments only in his twelfth and thirteenth years in office. What is more, Andropov was quickly accorded the kind of media fanfare not given Brezhnev until much later in his tenure. He was hailed as an "outstanding leader of the Leninist type" and his statements and "instructions" on both foreign and domestic issues were treated as the authoritative pronouncements of the leadership.

Andropov differed from his predecessors on another score: the brevity of his rule. He had a history of illnesses before November 1982, and at age sixty-eight was by much the oldest person ever to be made General Secretary, exceeding Brezhnev's age at accession by ten years and Khrushchev's by nine. We eventually learned from the posthumous medical bulletin that Andropov's kidneys failed, and dialysis treatment was begun, in February 1983. Soon after this he began missing public functions and appearing, when he did show up, gaunt and with shaking hands. He was last seen in public August 18, 1983. Though he is stated to have continued tending to party business until January 1984, his work routine was irregular and he was unable to attend key political events. He died February 9, 1984, and was buried beside Brezhnev in Red Square.

While the Politburo's exact motives in choosing Andropov in 1982 were never divulged, it is most doubtful that they intended a radical break with the status quo. However accurate the early reports of Andropov's taste for Western whiskey and jazz, he was a stickler for ideological propriety and on all essential points a product and defender of the mainstream political culture of the Soviet Union. In his meager formal training and long career in party administration, he resembled closely the typical official of his generation and the pair of *apparatchiki*, Brezhnev and Khrushchev, who preceded him.

Nonetheless, Andropov did differ from the norm in certain ways. His years in the KGB alone, the longest term as chief in its history, made him the first Soviet leader to have had prior custody of the secret police, and he had acquitted himself there, in Brezhnev's words, in a "clean and irreproachable" way that indicated he could be trusted with even greater power.[1] As a general point, Andropov had amassed much greater prior experience in Moscow, of all kinds, than previous bosses. He had been twenty-seven years in central administration, whereas Brezhnev and Khrushchev had but a dozen years between them and were fundamentally products of the provincial party machine. As the first leader since Stalin never to have been first secretary of a regional party organization, Andropov had limited experience with the day-in-day-out firefighting and juggling of production timetables that are the quintessence of local party work. His world had been that of high-level party, government, and security officials. He was more attuned than most Soviet politicians to the ideas and knowledge generated by the research institutes and think tanks that abound in the capital, and he had had unusual exposure to foreign affairs and the international environment.

Andropov had also been known as a man of urbanity, incorruptibility, and some compassion. That he was capable of serving in the KGB at all— or, as Soviet leader, of callously defending the September 1983 downing of an unarmed Korean airliner by Soviet interceptors, with the loss of 269 lives—was a reminder that he put the interests of the regime above all others. The fact remains, however, that he was perceived in some intellectual and professional circles as "the most educated and progressive party figure."[2] He clearly was persuaded by 1982 that Soviet problems had accumulated to the point that something had to be done in the interests of both the party and the population.

What, then, did Andropov accomplish with his power? Certainly, those Soviets and Westerners optimistic about political and ideological liberalization after Brezhnev were sorely disappointed. There was some opening up of political reporting and debate, in forms such as the new weekly communiqués on Politburo meetings and the publication of franker readers' letters and specialist articles in the Soviet press. Andropov also denounced stage-managed public meetings and called in nebulous terms for the "further democratization" of the political process; and in June 1983 legislation was passed providing for some worker participation in industrial management. On balance, though, the Andropov leadership tightened up rather than slackened state controls over the individual. There was a renewed drive against dissent, further restrictions on the arts, and a broad campaign for "socialist discipline," as Andropov called it, in all areas of life.

But this is far from the whole story. Yuri Andropov also set in motion the selective reform of policies and structures allowed to ossify and lose effectiveness under Brezhnev. To be sure, concrete changes (to be discussed in Chapter 4) were slow and deliberate, a pace seemingly dictated by Andropov's estimate of the political situation as much as by his health. He took pains to reassure conservative elements that sudden moves would not be taken and the contribution of loyal communists would not be slighted, telling party veterans that "not a single valuable grain" of their experience would be forgotten.[3]

Still, there is no mistaking that Andropov varied markedly from the 1964–82 baseline in terms of style and definition of the condition of the Soviet system. Gone was the air of sanctimonious self-congratulation common in the rhetoric of Brezhnev's day; it was replaced by an accent on the regime's backlog of problems. Andropov urged the party "to see the facts as they are" and "not to embellish anything" in diagnosing the USSR's ills. He stated without embarrassment that he personally had "no ready-made recipes" for resolving Soviet difficulties. What the country needs, he declared, is a period of self-appraisal and mending in which past oversights and errors are made up for and the way prepared for future advances: "We must soberly realize where we find ourselves. To jump forward would mean to take on unrealistic objectives; to dwell on our accomplishments would mean not to take advantage of all that we possess. What is demanded of us today is to see our society in its real dynamics, with all of its possibilities and needs."[4]

Andropov decried the passivity and unexamined habits that interfere with domestic progress, in particular the tendency to gloss over the disparity between theory and practice, between words and deeds. In this spirit, he flayed corruption among officials, shirkers in the work force, and hypocritical and ritualized propaganda campaigns. He repudiated the long-ignored 1961 Communist Party Program, which brims with overblown and unfulfillable Khrushchev-era promises, and called for adoption of a new one.

Andropov also struck a more cooly analytic note by praising rational inquiry and science as a guide to action. Within the framework of Marxism-Leninism, he promoted a new Soviet commitment to objective study of, and serious experimentation with, social and economic problems: "To be frank about it, we to this time have not studied to a sufficient extent the society in which we live and work and have not completely uncovered the laws peculiar to it, especially the economic ones. Therefore, we are often forced to act . . . by way of the extremely irrational method of trial and error." As part of the search for what he termed "an integrated strategy of social development," he advocated, far more than any earlier head of the party, learning from the successes and failures of other communist lands.[5]

Andropov's comments on specific issues ranged far and wide, from ideology and ethics to foreign relations, literature, the school system, health care and occupational safety, pollution, housing, the problems of the aged and of disaffected youth, nationality and language policy, and even to Soviet sport. He gave top billing, however, to the Soviet Union's stalled economy. Not only were his observations about all economic sectors more biting than Brezhnev's, but he also attributed the overall problem to poor leadership and policy and not just the peccadilloes of individual bureaucrats and workers. The country now has to devise, according to Andropov, "measures capable of giving greater scope of action to the colossal creative forces walled up in our economy."[6]

Andropov was adamant that such moves be "carefully prepared and realistic" and not flout the central precepts of socialism. But he made it equally plain that, as he put it in his last public speech, he wanted major decisions (*krupnyye resheniya*) on the economy, not another bout of the minimal reforms that typified the Brezhnev period: "We cannot be satisfied with our pace in shifting the economy onto the rails of intensive development. . . . It is obvious that in looking for ways to resolve new tasks we were not energetic enough, that not infrequently we resorted to half-measures and could not overcome the accumulated inertia quickly enough. Now we must make up for our neglect." This would require, he said, "changes in planning, management, and the economic mechanism" by the beginning of the next five-year plan in January 1986. As of his final statement on domestic policy, a message read to the Central Committee on his behalf in December 1983, Andropov was sticking to this schedule, admonishing against complacency over the economy's improved showing in 1983 and saying that the steps already taken were "only a beginning."[7]

Chernenko and Beyond

The selection of Konstantin Ustinovich Chernenko to succeed Andropov as General Secretary was apparently not an easy decision, for it took four days to announce, twice as long as for Andropov. It in no way settled the longer-term leadership issue. Chernenko, at seventy-two years of age (four years older than Andropov in 1982) and in uncertain health (reputed to have emphysema and perhaps other ailments), can only be an interim leader.

This white-haired son of Siberian peasants has remarkably few qualifications for holding one of the most powerful jobs in the world. Chernenko's formal education is limited to two years in the party's higher school and a correspondence degree from a teacher's college, earned when he was forty-two. He is a dull and mumbling public speaker, though some foreign statesmen say he is more animated in private. His career reaches back to the late 1920s (he joined the party in 1931, the same year as Brezhnev) and has been spent entirely in party propaganda and organization work. Incredibly, he had never before February 1984 run a major Soviet organization on his own. In the provinces and in Moscow, he had always been a supporting player.

It was Chernenko's good fortune that the individual he happened to support was Leonid Brezhnev. The two men's paths crossed in the republic of Moldavia in the early 1950s, and from 1960 on Chernenko acted as Brezhnev's office manager, troubleshooter, and confidant in Moscow. It was a sign of Brezhnev's growing authority (though not necessarily Chernenko's) when Chernenko was made head of the Central Committee's general department (which handles internal party communications) in 1965, a national party secretary in 1976, and a member of the Politburo two years later. Chernenko's power increased as Brezhnev's health worsened, the ailing leader's trust enabling him to nose out other Brezhnev cronies such as Andrei Kirilenko. Brezhnev is rumored even to have considered retiring from one or more of his positions in Chernenko's favor.

After being bested by Andropov in November 1982, Chernenko seemed politically orphaned and designated for retirement. As senior party secretary in the ideological realm, he was shorn of the patronage powers he had enjoyed from 1976 to 1982 and was far removed from the economic decisions that most interested Andropov. His major acts were to nominate

Andropov for his big appointments and to deliver a long-winded speech demanding ideological and cultural conformity in June 1983.

When Andropov's early enfeeblement and death unexpectedly gave Chernenko a second crack at the leadership, he did not waste it. His chief assets were doubtless his familiarity and the certainty that his rule would be brief. The choice defers passing on the leadership to a member of the younger political generation—who might rule for fifteen or twenty years—and gives the Politburo an occasion within several years to examine the question anew. That Chernenko won without the assistance of Brezhnev, the man to whom he previously owed everything, testifies to inner reserves, toughness, and a political dexterity not previously apparent in his career. Perhaps, his uninspiring public personality notwithstanding, there is a kernel of truth to Brezhnev's characterization of Chernenko as a "convinced fighter" for his beliefs who has "demonstrated an ability to win people over" to his point of view.[8]

Will the Soviet Union under Chernenko's transitional leadership lapse into the unimaginative conservatism that prevailed under his mentor? While by no means impossible, this is not a likely development for several reasons. First, the country's course is not to be set by Chernenko alone. Ironically, Andropov, who at first seemed to offer strong personal leadership, left behind a Politburo that probably functions as a more genuinely collegial body today than it ever has. It jointly made day-to-day decisions during Andropov's year of failing health, and one can assume that the substance of its decisions will not much change under Chernenko's chairmanship. He would need considerable time to reverse its course—more time than he probably has.

A second point is that Chernenko himself may well be more receptive to innovative policies than most Western commentary would suggest. There is evidence that he was trying to distance himself from Brezhnev prior to the latter's death. One survey of Chernenko's writings and speeches at that time found that he had "sought the support of progressive, reform-minded elements within the party" and appeared determined to prove that he was not a Brezhnev clone.[9] While Chernenko's economic ideas have been fuzzy, he seems to have favored some attempt to reduce overcentralization and promote greater initiative at lower levels. He has long been the most prominent advocate within the Soviet hierarchy of closer contact between the regime and the population. As party secretary, he sponsored the establishment of public opinion polling centers within the party and greater responsiveness to citizens' letters and complaints. In 1980–81 he warned strenuously that a Solidarity-type crisis could engulf the Soviet system if its leaders failed to allay mass frustration because of economic and social failures.

Chernenko's very adaptability as a politician will also impel him to carry on rather than abort Andropov's modest reforms. Whatever his initial opinion of the late leader's policies—and there is no hint that he opposed any of them—he must now function in a climate greatly influenced by them. Andropov's halting changes and plain speaking about Soviet troubles raised public and elite hopes of improvement, especially in the economy. Although Chernenko hypothetically could thumb his nose at these aspirations, his record suggests he will not. His biography makes it unlikely that he will come up with a fresh program of his own, but he is not apt to abrogate Andropov's policies either. Most likely, he will preside over a collective leadership committed to searching for solutions to domestic problems, more or less along the lines preferred by Andropov, and to an orderly transition of power to younger men.

Chernenko's early statements as head of the party conveyed exactly this kind of orientation. Heaping praise on Andropov (while making no reference whatever to Brezhnev), they vowed an extension of Andropov's policies: "To continue and through collective efforts to move forward the work begun under Yuri Vladimirovich—that is the best means of rendering our due to his memory, of achieving continuity in policy." In his general outlook, Chernenko has sounded uncannily like his predecessor, at times even borrowing his precise words and phrases. And he has stressed that he plans to persevere with measures such as the 1983 crackdown on bribery and embezzlement, and that there should be no "illusions" about this being a short-lived campaign.

Concerning the central Soviet problem of lagging economic growth, Chernenko has echoed Andropov by referring to a need for "a serious restructuring of our economy's management system, of our entire economic mechanism" and professing that work on this "has only begun" since November 1982. He has specifically endorsed Andropov's notions about increasing material rewards for productivity as well as the major experiments in industrial management and planning begun in 1984, saying these will eventually be the basis for more comprehensive reforms. Again, he has cautioned against the conclusion that Andropov's death means the abandonment of change, scoring "any kind of conservatism and stagnation" in economic approaches and reprimanding unnamed skeptics "who do not at all wish to reckon with changed conditions, with the new requirements of life."[10]

His tenure, as it progresses, will reveal whether Chernenko intends to translate his words into action and if he will have more time and strength than Andropov to do so. Given his interim status, it is not premature to think of future leadership change. Beyond Chernenko there lurks yet another Soviet succession. Much about the result hinges on the manner and time of his leaving. If Chernenko dies, is incapacitated, or retires within a year or two, the nod could go one more time to another provisional leader from roughly his age cohort: perhaps Viktor Grishin (born in 1914), the durable Moscow party boss, or Defense Minister Dmitri Ustinov (born 1908), who has strong credentials as a patriot and economic manager. Such a person could serve for several years in a caretaker capacity before yielding in a final stage to a considerably younger candidate.

The longer Chernenko hangs on, however, the better the odds that a more junior individual will come to the fore directly. Precedent gives the advantage to the two Politburo-ranking secretaries passed over in February 1984. The younger of these, Mikhail Gorbachev (born in 1931), must now be considered the prohibitive favorite. Whether coincidentally or not, Gorbachev made his career in the Stavropol area of the North Caucasus, where Andropov was born and took his vacations; Gorbachev went directly from being first secretary there to the post of national party secretary for agriculture in 1978 and a seat on the Politburo in 1980. In the spring of 1983, he was assigned top-level responsibility for personnel matters, managing thereafter to place associates in a number of major positions.[11] He soon increased his participation in foreign affairs, and upon Andropov's death he took charge of ideological policy as well. Gorbachev may soon shed some of his many duties; but as things now stand he is in effect second secretary of the party and enviably positioned to make a leadership bid should Chernenko lose his grip. He may even have the position locked up already as the result of a deal struck within the Politburo.

Gorbachev is the first lawyer to sit in the Politburo since the Lenin era, has a second degree as an agronomist, speaks passable English, and has impressed foreigners (as in his May 1983 visit to Canada) with his knowledgeability and wit. He has the reputation in Moscow of shrewdness and open-mindedness about economic experimentation and catering to the Soviet consumer, and one can only assume that his becoming Andropov's right-hand man testifies to agreement between them on the broad necessity for moderate reform. Gorbachev also makes tough-sounding statements about crime, discipline, and the work ethic—the very sort that would assuage conservatives' fears—and seems to have had a good rapport with the late chief ideologist of the regime, Suslov.

After Gorbachev, the most likely possibility is Grigori Romanov, the dour Leningrad party boss brought into the Central Committee Secretariat in June 1983, with responsibility for defense industry, machine building, and perhaps some other economic questions as well. Romanov might appeal to many in the party as a compromise between Gorbachev and an older man. A wounded war veteran, born in 1923, he is about halfway in age between Chernenko and Gorbachev and has been a Politburo member for twice as long as Gorbachev. Although he has not received especially prominent press play, he appears to have had some success in promoting former Leningrad colleagues.[12] Romanov has a standard engineering education (done at night school), has worked in defense production (in shipbuilding), and is reported by Leningraders and the few Westerners to have met him to be a strong Russian nationalist and a stiff-necked conservative on cultural questions. On the other hand, he has long advocated more imaginative efforts to raise industrial productivity and has voiced an acute interest in urban blue-collar workers and their discontents, a qualification that may be of greater relevance after the Solidarity earthquake in Poland. Under him, Leningrad was a leading center for urban and regional planning and for institutional reorganization to bring about technological innovation.[13]

The Dynamics of Succession

The names of other possible successors could be raised — of Vitali Vorotnikov (the new premier of the Russian Republic), for example, or of Vladimir Dolgikh or Nikolai Ryzhkov (party secretaries in the industrial field) — but conjecture of this sort has a limited value. We may be better served by some general observations on the dynamics of the ongoing succession process and its likely effect on the Soviet political system. For the present, Chernenko is at the helm of both party and state — having been elected ceremonial head of state in April 1984 — but it is doubtful that he yet has much unilateral decision power. The next transition is fast approaching and, what with the dizzying stakes and the absence in a single-party dictatorship of a binding code governing leadership selection, there is no guarantee that it will go as smoothly as in November 1982 or February 1984. In any event, Chernenko's successor tomorrow, like Chernenko today or Andropov yesterday, will discover that getting there is only half the battle. He will still be left struggling with the task of building and exercising authority *after* obtaining the peak post.[14]

Any General Secretary begins his term surrounded by colleagues who are in no way beholden to him for their positions, and that is his first great problem. He has dealt with it, in years gone by, in large part by manipulating appointments, a right Stalin made a major prerogative of the General Secretary in the 1920s. He has settled long-time friends and associates in sensitive posts at top and intermediate levels, and has also used purges and his substantial ability to rig intraparty elections to recruit new supporters and pack decision-making bodies with them, up to and including the Central Committee and Politburo. Brezhnev, in addition to making selective use of these methods, was able to win a further measure of support among the broad office-holding class merely by ceding to most of them security of tenure.

In the 1980s, these customary strategies are no longer as promising or feasible as before. The last technique was a one-time-only device: now that stable tenure has come to be accepted by many officials as a normal condition, the post-Brezhnev leader cannot hope to reap political benefit from it. As for favoritism toward old cronies and new followers, this is now made more awkward by collective decision making at the top. The General Secretary can subvert oligarchy only gradually, for he must take care not to raise the hackles of his peers. The changing nature of Soviet political and administrative careers blunts the sword of patronage still further. Particularly under Brezhnev's tutelage, the mobile party generalist, easily reprogrammed, has given way to a much more professional and specialized official, who is expected to be technically competent and seasoned in the particular agency or region in which he works. Typically, he is promoted from within, thus posing a serious obstacle to the Kremlin patron who seeks to colonize outlying parts of the bureaucracy by carrying out frequent shakeups and sending in his loyalists.[15] High-ranking politicians, as they advance along more structured career paths, also acquire a smaller and less diverse "tail" of clients, as the Soviets say, than was true previously. Andropov was a forerunner of this trend. He did not have the strongholds in several different regions and hierarchies that Brezhnev and Khrushchev had before him, and he was the first incoming boss since Lenin not to have had as his most recent post that of senior party secretary overseeing cadres selection (a task performed in 1982 by Chernenko). Chernenko has a more traditional career profile, but because of his long dependence on Brezhnev he seems to have very few close associates of his own.[16] Chernenko's successor, assuming he is from the younger group, is likely to have even shorter political coattails. Gorbachev, for example, spent his entire administrative career up to 1978 in his native Stavropol region; Romanov had never worked outside of Leningrad before June 1983.

This is not to say, however, that Chernenko or the next General Secretary will have compunctions about using his influence over personnel to brace his political position and help execute his policies. Far from it: this very kind of operation will be a prime feature of Soviet politics throughout the 1980s, as the multi-stage succession is played out and the aging Soviet elite rejuvenated. Andropov began on this front with an early warning to officials who "simply do not know how to work," contained in a speech, like all his addresses as leader, missing any reference to Brezhnev's maxim of "respect for cadres."[17] During his fifteen months in power, senior positions changed hands at a pace not seen in two decades.

Early changes at the top of the pyramid were gradual enough to demonstrate that Andropov had to tread delicately, but without question they greatly strengthened his political hand even as his physical strength ebbed. One outsider (Vorotnikov) was brought into the Politburo, two Politburo candidate members (Geidar Aliyev and Mikhail Solomentsev) were co-opted to full membership, and there was one new Politburo candidate (Viktor Chebrikov, the KGB chief), one Politburo member given the rank of secretary (Romanov), and two new secretaries. Only a single Politburo member (Kirilenko) was retired—one member and two candidates died in office—and holdovers from the Brezhnev faction such as Chernenko and Nikolai Tikhonov were still conspicuously in place when Andropov died. At middle grades, the results were more impressive. Soon after attaining Politburo membership in late 1982, Geidar Aliyev was promoted from party first secretary in the southern republic of Azerbaidzhan to First Deputy Chairman of the Council of Ministers in Moscow. A former KGB official renowned in Azerbaidzhan for his purging of the corrupt and the inept, Aliyev busied himself with a limited housecleaning in the state bureaucracy. In the party apparatus, the responsibility fell to one Yegor Ligachev, plucked from an obscure Siberian post, installed as head of the cadres department in April 1983, and made the national secretary directly handling party organization eight months later, presumably as Andropov's handpicked lieutenant.[18]

During the brief reign of Andropov, changes affected the chiefs of six Central Committee departments (for party cadres, propaganda, economic coordination, foreign cadres, science and education, and confidential documents) and of the party's chancellery, 23 members of the Council of Ministers, and 20 regional party bosses of Central Committee rank. Of the just over 300 surviving members of the 1981 Central Committee, 44 were demoted or retired under Andropov (most of them replaced by younger men), 29 were promoted, and 3 were reassigned to unknown posts. Counting the three members who died in the same period, total turnover in that body occurred at an annual rate of about 20 percent, not a sweeping purge but roughly triple the rate of the 1970s. Some former Brezhnev protegés—among them Interior Minister Nikolai Shchelokov and Ignati Novikov, the overlord of the construction industry—were among the victims, and Shchelokov and another friend of Brezhnev were expelled from the Central Committee (and evidently from the party as well) in June 1983, the first time this has happened since 1964. Officials with several specific backgrounds—notably service in the state planning organs and in defense industry—have fared especially well in the promotion sweepstakes, suggesting that Andropov was attempting to win favor in these quarters and use personnel from them to extend his control.[19]

Chernenko may want to decelerate the reshuffling of officials somewhat, yet he cannot afford to halt it. Even if he were to try, this would have only a temporary impact. There is no reason to doubt that, as new leaders act to consolidate their power, change in personnel will occur at a brisk clip.

The chief implication of the changed circumstances of Soviet elite politics is not at all, then, that machine politics will be eschewed by the General Secretary. Rather, it is that maneuvers in this realm will not be enough to build and maintain the leader's authority. Lacking prior career associations with most of the individuals he helps up the ladder, the party head, be it Chernenko or his successor, will tend to form with them only the weakest of patronage bonds, that of mere appointment.[20] Unless the painfully evolved rules of politics within the elite are re-crafted, the leader will have to refrain from violence in making his changes—in fact, under a new procedure, most of the senior officials retired under Andropov and Chernenko have been publicly thanked by the Politburo for their service. The leader will also have to weigh the opinions of his Kremlin colleagues in wielding the patronage weapon and, to a far greater extent than a generation ago, the merit and experience of candidates as well. Most (though not all) of those promoted since Brezhnev's death have actually been drawn from the same hierarchy or territory as the person replaced.[21]

Several conclusions follow. The first involves the way the General Secretary buoys his authority. If he—and his open or concealed rivals, if there be any—find the old levers of patronage wanting, they will look elsewhere. Soviet leaders now need more than before to win over and retain supporters by other means, in particular through substantive policy. This is precisely what Andropov did after November 1982, acting as a spokesman and energizer as much as a backroom operator. He at first used some mildly unorthodox means to get his message across (including, when he was still on his feet, an apparently unrehearsed appearance at a Moscow machine tool plant in January 1983 and a solo article in the party's theoretical journal), then reverted to the traditional kinds of executive action and exhortation that probably will be preferred by Chernenko.

A second point is also underlined by Andropov's early performance. Admittedly, because the head of the party can move only slowly to fill the leadership with his dependents and will never be able to behave as an autocrat in the mold of Stalin or even Khrushchev, Kremlin politics is apt to be "a politics . . . of accommodation rather than one of winner-take-all."[22] Nevertheless, the General Secretary who plays hard and with his best cards is still capable of coming away from the table with more than the other players. His sense of mission, timing, and skill in manipulating the political situation may be as important in shaping the outcome of leadership politics as the size of his clientele. Brezhnev, it must not be forgotten, grew more conservative the longer he was in office and the more of his own men he was able to promote: the more power he had, the less inclined he was to use it. Andropov seemed to see his role otherwise, as an advocate of moderate change, and to believe, moreover, that this was what his constituency desired. His political success showed that under present Soviet conditions—after years of worsening domestic difficulties and dithering leadership—people do want a move away from Brezhnev-vintage conservatism. This being the case, Chernenko, or Gorbachev, or Romanov has every incentive to play to that mood and to make good on promises of prudent reform.

Generational Change and the Itch for Improvement

Behind the jousting for high office, another great change is occurring: this in the entire Soviet elite, where a massive shift in generations is under way. Whatever is decided in the Kremlin in the several years ahead, the larger transition in leadership, which will continue throughout the decade, is likely to make the regime increasingly amenable to moderate reform. It is lifting into power younger individuals more critical of Soviet failings than their elders are and with more of an itch for improvement.

Generational change has been staved off for as long as humanly possible by the old ones in office, officials born in the first two decades of the twentieth century and in many cases before 1910. They are the beneficiaries of Stalin's bloody prewar purges and of the vacuum the slaughter created within the Soviet political and administrative elite. Catapulted into positions of great responsibility in their thirties or younger, these individuals have maintained a near-stranglehold on top office for decades and only began to loosen it in the 1970s. They have used their long years in power to justify staying there, and their role at climactic points in Soviet history like the industrialization drive and World War II as a source of moral authority. It has been obligatory, one party executive has explained, "to display the maximum of sensitivity" in broaching the pensioning-off of even poorly qualified members of the older generation. "Often it is difficult to blame such a person for lagging behind, for not studying. [He points to] his difficult youth, the war, his important assignments, [how] he himself barely noticed how his life flew by as he worried about things necessary to the party and state."[23] No amount of "sensitivity" sufficed to get Leonid Brezhnev (born in 1906) or his elderly Politburo colleagues to vacate office voluntarily.

The handing-over of power has been further delayed by the lingering effects of World War II. Men born approximately between the 1917 Russian Revolution and the mid-1920s bore the brunt of the sacrifices at the front, and those who survived were often cheated of the advanced technical training needed for the best political and managerial posts. As a result, the wartime generation has served as a poor bridge between men in the age bracket of Brezhnev, Chernenko, and Andropov and those born in the second half of the 1920s or the 1930s and reared under greatly different conditions.[24]

The arrival of politicians born after the mid-1920s and now in their forties and fifties—some call them the postwar generation, others the post-Stalin generation—is imminent. Predictably, the last to register the change is the party high command, where in the spring of 1984 only two Politburo members out of twelve (Gorbachev and Vorotnikov), one candidate member of six (Eduard Shevardnadze), and one of five non-Politburo secretaries (Ryzhkov) were under sixty.[25] The average age of the 1984 Politburo members, candidates, and secretaries was sixty-eight. For the 1981 Central Committee, the most recent to be elected, it was sixty-five in 1984. Individuals from the postwar generation, however, already fill most leadership chairs in the regional party organs and are entering senior positions in economic ministries, the military and KGB, and the foreign policy establishment. Eighty-five of 319 members of the 1981 Central Committee, including 44 of 88 novice members, were born after 1925; so were 71 of 151 candidate members, among them 54 of 90 new ones. Only the most unlikely defiance of the laws of biology could keep the postwar generation from becoming a large majority in the Central Committee by the end of the 1980s. If succession-inspired promotions expedite the process, this point may be reached at the next scheduled party congress in 1986.

But what is the significance of the turnover of generations? Will the new leaders govern the Soviet Union any differently? There will be, to start with, a change in physical and mental vigor. Even if younger men mirrored all their mentors' values, greater energy would enable them to carry out the same policies more effectively. Thus, for example, one Soviet survey of plant directors in the Sverdlovsk region discovered that managers older than sixty, regardless of their "great experience and enormous knowledge," find it "more and more difficult with the passage of the years to lead production collectives." The article, which echoed so well problems at the summit of Soviet leadership, recommended that the title of honorary director be conferred on reluctant retirees, with a stipend attached, and that they be replaced by younger, more aggressive persons.[26] If sixty (the legal pension age for Soviet men) is the age at which the manager of a factory buckles under the work load, one can readily imagine the difficulty with which bodies such as the Politburo and Central Committee, responsible for running the entire country, and where average ages are in the middle and late sixties, discharge their duties.

The impatience and therefore, perhaps, the effect of a new generation are apt to be all the greater when they have waited a long time for the opportunity. In the Soviet case, however, there is an odd wrinkle. When it looked at the deputies of the plant directors, the Sverdlovsk study reported the "not quite normal phenomenon" of understudies who are only a few years younger than their superiors and are their natural successors but have been kept in the wings for so long that they have lost their élan. "As a result, the directors are left without bold deputies, deputies with initiative. . . . This increases the load on the people at the top, who are already at the 'heart attack level' of leadership." Some directors, the authors added, have only themselves to thank because, "fearing competition from able assistants, they themselves choose passive ones." If new managers were to be dynamic, the study concluded, recruiters would have to skip over the weary and demoralized second tier and go straight to the ranks of the younger, better educated, and more enterprising chief engineers of the factories.[27] As many Soviet readers would have gathered, this portrait of industry is a fetching microcosm of the whole Soviet regime of the late Brezhnev period: aging bosses convinced of their indispensability, unchallenged by lackluster lieutenants, but afraid to gamble on the youth and talent an echelon or two below. If the analogy holds true, it makes especially good sense to anticipate a reinvigoration of the political system when the postwar generation of officials—the rough equivalent of the Sverdlovsk chief engineers—finally claims its patrimony.

The arrival of the postwar generation should, therefore, be reflected in the execution of established policy. Yet, will it also lead to changes in the direction of policy? Will the new rulers have beliefs or priorities any different from the old? A political generation may differ from its predecessors either by deliberately rejecting their policies or by gradually leaving them behind as it puts into effect attitudes acquired by its members during their maturation.[28] Both inclinations can be found in the USSR's postwar political generation. Because the old guard has retained power for so long, the two tendencies are difficult to disentangle from one another.

The formative experiences of the postwar generation have demonstrably differed in several respects from those of the outgoing leaders. For one thing, younger officials had no hand in founding the Soviet system's basic political and economic institutions. Brezhnev participated in the brutal collectivization of agriculture at the end of the 1920s, as apparently did Chernenko; and Brezhnev, Chernenko, and Andropov helped bring under Soviet control non-Russian territories (Moldavia and Karelia) annexed by Stalin during the war. The coming generation had no part in these events. Trained to take the basic features of the Soviet order as given, it seems more relaxed about the possibilities of evolutionary improvement and less frightened that moderate change will destabilize the whole structure. The postwar group is also too young to have been implicated in Stalin's witch hunts and killings, having entered political life in most cases after his death. Unthreatened by de-Stalinization, it had less reason than older colleagues to be traumatized by Khrushchev's rowdy reforms. Conversely, it had less cause to be satisfied with the lead-footed conservatism of the Brezhnev years. The setbacks of the 1970s, coming at the prime of these men's careers, seem to have had a more wrenching impact on them. Unlike their elders, they know the consequences of present failures will be in their laps.

The maturing political generation is also quite different in its material expectations. Its standard of living, beginning around 1950, has steadily risen for all or most of these people's lives. Whereas for the senior generation, "all this was a novelty — refrigerators, vacuum cleaners, separate apartments, hot water," for them, especially those born after the mid-1930s, the features of a modern consumer society "are all natural, all a norm of life."[29] The emerging generation's material and other expectations have also been heightened by formal education, acquired without interruption by war or work and without discrimination on the basis of class origin. By and large, they are both technically and in a general cultural sense considerably more sophisticated than their predecessors. A far larger percentage of the younger executives have an advanced degree in the law, economics, or another social science. For this reason, they tend more than the senior group, almost all of whom had engineering backgrounds, to be skeptical of narrowly technical solutions to economic or social problems. Younger men have come of age in the least repressive intellectual climate in Soviet history. They have often had at least indirect contact with the external world and seem to presume that, unless politics or core ideological principles determine otherwise, the Soviet Union should draw on foreign knowledge and practice.

It would be preposterous to expect the postwar generation to turn the Soviet Union upside down. It shares with the veterans of earlier marches fundamental values — faith in one-party rule and the state-owned economy, identification with Soviet achievements, insistence on the USSR's status as a world power — and a general assumption that its best interests lie with the existing Soviet system. It could not be called "liberal" in the usual Western meaning of the word, for it seems little attracted to the notion of the primacy of individual rights and is in many ways as authoritarian as its predecessors. Nor is the post-Stalin generation internally homogeneous. There are significant divisions within it — ideological, programmatic, bureaucratic, territorial, and so forth — just as there were in previous age groups. Its capture of the political commanding heights will neither dissolve these tensions nor reverse basic beliefs and operating assumptions. What we are likely to see, rather than destabilization or black-to-white change, is a reshading of the greys, a gradual shift in the political class's center of gravity.

An itch for improvement has worked its way into the attitudes of many members of the successor generation. It can be detected in their treatment of specific policy issues in public debate and, to the limited extent that foreigners have access, in private discussion as well. If one looks, as an illustration, at speeches delivered before the 1981 party congress by the regional party first secretaries, one notices measurable generational differences. Party secretaries born in 1926 or later paid much less attention to ideological questions than the older secretaries. They were considerably less likely to urge old-fashioned extensive development of either agriculture (usually entailing big outlays for irrigation) or industry (building new factories) or to discourse on the need for better central management of the economy. The younger secretaries were instead more interested in pushing innovative, intensive solutions to economic problems (involving research and development, retooling, updating of infrastructure, better work incentives, and the like). Party officials from the postwar generation were almost twice as likely as older ones at the conclave to bring up the need for improving consumer welfare via housing construction, better personal services and environmental protection, and production of more household goods and food. When they mentioned consumer satisfaction, it was often in the context of boosting worker motivation and productivity. The younger men also devoted twice as much attention to one specific strategy for decentralization of decision making, namely, the beefing up of local coordination of economic and social development at the expense of the Moscow planners and ministerial head offices.[30]

The desire for improvement comes through as clearly in the broad discussions of social and economic problems found in the Soviet media. Members of the postwar generation openly confess that the system of economic management developed in the 1930s "has sunk deep roots . . . into the imagination of the administrative apparatus, many of whose officials consider it the sole possible one," and that the resulting myopia has prevented many older officials from facing the system's shortcomings. Times have changed, many younger members of the elite were saying in the late Brezhnev years, and policies and methods must keep step with them. A department head in the party's Academy of Social Sciences put it this way in 1982: "Today, in the 1980s, economic and social progress cannot be achieved by the old methods, by the ones that a relatively short time ago brought decent results. The lack of understanding of this, attempts to work in the old ways under new conditions, and setting store exclusively by the experience of the past serve as a supportive medium for inertia in administration and economic thought."[31]

Younger officials and scholars are more critical than older ones of weaknesses in the traditional economic formula, such as overcentralization and obsession with year-end production totals. They frequently note that "slogans and salutations are insufficient" to move the country forward and how much there is a need to punch through the crust of custom and routine: "Improvement of economic planning and management . . . demands a creative approach, a certain boldness, and experimentation. Otherwise, we cannot overcome inertness and stagnation in economic work, we cannot get away from traditions and habits that have had their day." They sometimes evince a restlessness with the painstaking process of consultation and deference to cautious experts emblematic of the Brezhnev years. One regional party secretary writes admiringly of a comrade, a construction executive, who pushed through a new building method against "the objections of influential specialists who did not want to take a risk." The construction boss was praised for attempting something new, and his success was said to underscore the importance of the party holding cadres to account for keeping pace with society's demands, "regardless of past services."[32]

Individuals who came to political maturity after Stalin's death also appear more galled by lame apologies for Soviet difficulties—the kind found in the jingles and stale slogans of Soviet ideologists. They show less respect (and sometimes none at all) for excusing Soviet shortcomings as minor aberrations from a healthy mean, the fault of one scapegoat leader, or vestiges of pre-1917 history. In the past several years, caustic comments have appeared in the press on the hoary theory that problems like crime, corruption, ethnic conflict, and the housing shortage are "survivals of the past" with no basis in modern Soviet society. "When we speak of 'survivals,'" one critic said a few months before Brezhnev's death, "the impression is created that these phenomena are residual and insignificant," although in fact certain of the country's problems are not only persevering but (as with corruption) are noticeably worsening. Repetition of the old alibis, she continued, "oversimplifies the situation, unjustifiably idealizes real life, prevents us from seeing the full outlines and extent of [the problems], the overcoming of which is possible only as a result of the clear-headed definition of long-term strategy and tactics."[33]

Similarly, many in the postwar elite are talking about lost time and the possibility of a social deadlock or even decay unless real leadership is shown soon on the USSR's major problems. In a nutshell, they have been feeling and saying that, particularly under Brezhnev (a point that is made implicitly but unmistakably), there has been too much drift, too little decision, and too few answers to the nagging questions about the Soviet way of life. What does socialism mean a lifetime after the events that brought it into being? Where is guidance to be found when neither ideology nor precedent provides it? In the absence of honest answers from the party and state, says one legal scholar and party official, "practice is having to provide the answers independently," practice being the accidental concatenation of circumstances, personalities, and guesswork. Without timely and painful choices, "it will be necessary [in future] to do things over, to rebuild, to unlearn our acquired habits, that is, in a certain sense to turn around and start over. It does not have to be said what social costs could be connected with such a situation."[34] This foreboding about losing what they already have makes many in the Soviet Union, especially the up-and-coming members of the middle class, take more seriously the need for reforms.

The Military and the KGB

Two pillars of the Soviet establishment of particular interest in forecasting the future are the coercive elites: the armed forces, which have mainly a foreign mission; and the KGB, whose principal function is domestic political control. For both organizations, the Brezhnev period was one of budgetary prosperity and increased status and influence. In 1981–82, the almost simultaneous coming to power of a former KGB chief in Moscow and, next door in Poland, a uniformed army general, encouraged some in the West to see the military and the security police as assuming a dominant role in the affairs of the Soviet Union and some of its allies. Is there any substance to this theory in the Soviet case? If not, how will the armed guardians of the regime affect Soviet politics and the prospects for change and reform?

There is no solid evidence that party-army-KGB relations were realigned during or by Andropov's rise to power. Some infer this realignment from Andropov's KGB background, from Defense Minister Ustinov's apparent support of him in November 1982, and from Andropov's and Ustinov's having been the first two speakers at Brezhnev's funeral. These are slender reeds on which to build a case. Andropov, in the final analysis, was a *party* politician, albeit one who put in a stint as the Politburo's man in the KGB. He would have been an also-ran in the leadership race without strong support in the party apparatus. Marshal Ustinov, likewise, was a prodigy in civilian administration (since age twenty-six a senior state and party official supervising arms production), long before becoming Minister of Defense over the heads of qualified military candidates in 1976. Ustinov, if he did indeed side with Andropov in 1982, was not necessarily speaking for the officer corps, and his attempt in a May 1983 article to fabricate a military reputation for Andropov was a transparent act of political opportunism at which many professional soldiers must have winced.[35]

By 1984, Ustinov was lauding another new leader, Chernenko. It is unlikely that a succession heavily influenced by the army or the KGB would have appointed Chernenko, who has no major connection with either. (Indeed, he is the first Soviet leader since Stalin not to have seen active duty in World War II. His only quasi-military service was in 1930–33 in the Soviet Border Guards.) Nor is either of the prime contenders for the next succession, Gorbachev or Romanov, known to have career associations with either organization. If the army and KGB did have such influence, one could expect a candidate with a professional military or KGB background to be at least a contender, if not the victor. This not being so, there is no good reason to suppose that the party's primacy as the foremost decision-making and governing entity has in any way diminished.

Under Andropov and Chernenko, it has still been the broadly representative organs of the Communist Party that set national priorities, hire and fire personnel, and control the budgetary purse strings. Military and KGB officers sit on the party's organs of decision, but as a small minority, consulted mainly on issues directly linked to their missions. As U.S.–Soviet relations have worsened of late, and arms control talks have foundered, the armed forces' mission has increased in visibility—hence events such as the two press conferences dominated by Marshal Nikolai Ogarkov, the Chief of the General Staff, which were expected on American television screens in the autumn of 1983. This, however, hardly proves that the military or the secret police are running the entire Soviet Union, as some plainly irresponsible Western commentary has suggested.

Were the power of the army or KGB to be much greater today than under Brezhnev, we would expect them to be receiving payoffs in terms of appointments—especially the KGB, which Andropov headed for fifteen years and where he would naturally have looked for trusted supporters to promote. With the military, there is not the slightest indication of this happening. For the KGB, it has been done only selectively. Only the Ministry of the Interior, the civilian police force under attack for corrupt practices, has been penetrated by KGB cadres to any significant extent—Andropov's immediate successor as KGB chief, Vitali Fedorchuk, was made head of the ministry in December 1982—yet even here the KGB has had to share prominence with new party organs in the ministry supervised by local party committees and headed by an official, Viktor Gladyshev, recruited directly from the Central Committee apparatus.[36] Alumni of several civilian organizations, notably Gosplan, the state planning committee, have been far more widely and highly placed since November 1982 than those of the KGB or army.

If, mind you, profound changes in Soviet politics were to occur under new leaders, the party-army-KGB triangle could be affected. Blanket re-Stalinization, for instance, would magnify the role of the secret police. Bitter factional conflict within the party might impel one or several of the warring groups to court the police or the military, as happened in China in the 1960s and, in a more limited way, in the Soviet Union shortly after

Stalin's death. If, more serious still, a deep political or economic crisis threatened the regime's control over the population, the party leadership would be tempted to enlist military or KGB aid to restore order and rebuild its authority. The more severe the challenge, the more likely that the army, which dwarfs the KGB in size, firepower, and prestige, would be seen as the redeemer. The culmination of such a process could conceivably be a replay of the 1981 events in Poland: appointment of a military officer as head of the party, imposition of martial law, and partial abdication of the discredited civilian party to the armed forces.[37]

None of these sea changes is at all apt to take place—although none is totally beyond the realm of possibility. The Soviet Union's political system, unlike Poland's, has powerful, built-in sources of stability. The chances of either the army or the KGB wanting to usurp civilian authority on their own initiative are slight because of their privileged position in pay, prestige, and the rest. The chances of an attempted coup are further reduced by the innate tension between the two agencies, rooted in military memories of Stalin's police-administered purges and in the KGB's role as a watchdog over the officer corps.[38] In thinking about the possibility of independent action by the KGB, the organization more likely to object strenuously to reformist changes, it is worth recalling that in the past it has not done well in impeding changes not to its taste. At Stalin's death in 1953, the police ran a vast internal empire, had millions of citizens in labor camps, and could make the most senior politician's knees tremble. All of this power, far exceeding that of the KGB today, was of no avail in preventing either de-Stalinization or the undoing of the secret police's autonomy.

There is a deep-seated consensus within the civilian party apparatus against any marked upgrading of KGB or military power. With regard to the secret police, this consensus has been often expressed. Even Andropov, when KGB chief, had harsh words for the "political adventurists" who headed the KGB's forerunners under Stalin. He quoted with approval a remark made about Felix Dzerzhinski, the founder of the original Cheka, commending him as "a great party man, observant of the law and modest, for whom the directive of the party was everything."[39] As the man signing party directives as General Secretary, Andropov was as committed as before to seeing that Dzerzhinski's example was minded, and his successors will surely not be much different.

As for the army, the refrain about civilian supremacy remains equally prominent. "The foundation of foundations of Soviet military development," Ustinov declared in late 1982, "is the leadership of the Communist Party. The significance of this leadership is under contemporary conditions growing even greater."[40] It is probably not a coincidence that reminders of the party's preeminence have been more frequent and more barbed since Wojciech Jaruzelski's imposition of martial law in Poland—a tocsin intended, one guesses, for any Soviet general who begins to fantasize. Party spokesmen have disparaged as "bourgeois" the idea "that any army, including a socialist army, is somehow a force that is 'above [social] classes,' an instrument for regulating the political relations of the entire nation." In a communist system, such a task is reserved to the party alone.[41]

Assuming no transformation of their relations with the regime, what can be anticipated of the KGB and the military command in the politics of the coming decade? The domestic role of the KGB will necessarily be bounded by its limited mandate. It is difficult to see it having much political voice on the USSR's crucial social and economic problems, for it does not have the expertise and finesse to help choose or reconcile intricate public policies. Its role as the party's enforcer will, however, remain for as long as the Soviet Union remains an authoritarian state, and could indeed become more important if moderate reform is adopted (as will be seen in the next chapter).

The army's place in the political equation is different. It cannot exercise a veto on basic questions, but it is no mere servant either. Given its size, its political contacts, its battlefield mystique, its association with Russian nationalism, and its status as the customer of the most dynamic branch of the economy, the military's views are listened to with respect.

Which way will the army lean? Would it support or oppose moderate reform? One clue comes from the changing scope of its operations. The Soviet officer corps has in the past been a strictly professional body, functioning behind a high wall of secrecy and possessing, together with its allies in the defense industry, a near-monopoly of the information relevant to making military decisions. This insularity has begun to erode in recent decades as the enterprise of building and managing military power has broadened. The military now more frequently finds itself in situations where it is only one of several qualified participants, sharing authority with other organizations beyond its partners in the armaments industry. The army's weapons systems depend increasingly on technologies coming out of civilian science and industry: new materials and alloys, hardware and software for communications and data processing, manufacturing and miniaturizing techniques, directed energy, and the like. The military must now work more closely with civilian diplomats (in arms control negotiations and in publicizing national security decisions), with nonmilitary institutes of international relations (which have begun to study U.S. military doctrine and the link between military power and foreign policy), with factory managers and local governments (on civil defense), and with school and young people's organizations (for paramilitary training and basic military education).

At the same time, the party leadership has become more interested in recruiting assistance from the military-industrial complex for lagging sectors of the civilian economy. In the late 1970s, military-related institutes and design bureaus were ordered to devote part of their time to help produce better machinery for use in industry at large.[42]

Where do military interests and the blurring of the civil-military boundary leave the army with respect to political change? As cultural conservatives deeply committed to the regime's stability, army officers will be unfriendly toward genuine political liberalization or hasty reforms of any genre. They will also have particular qualms about changes carried out at their expense—changes challenging their astronomical share of the state budget. Reductions in defense outlays will surely be considered by the regime in the 1980s whether or not more systematic reforms are pursued, although the final decision will hang as much on foreign policy as on domestic considerations (this will be explored in Chapter 5).

Notwithstanding its selfish concerns, the Soviet military is not necessarily an implacable enemy of reform. The adverse effects of budget cuts on military morale could be cushioned by going about them gradually and by mollifying the officer corps with higher salaries and pensions. As a practical matter, moderate reforms could be undertaken without chopping military expenditures at all. Most important, however, there are several positive reasons why the military might go along with a modest and well-buffered reform program even if its budget were cut.

First, military leaders are well aware that a stumbling Soviet economy is going to be less and less able to shoulder the burden of defense spending they have come to expect. Economic stagnation and crisis will force either a slowdown in Soviet military spending—as already occurred in the late 1970s, when the rate of expansion of the defense budget was pared to 2 percent from the previous 4 to 5 percent—or an increase in the military's share of the overall pie. If the army's slice expands, the rate of growth of the pie will eventually shrink further, making less available for military use. Recent statements by Soviet military leaders indicate that they understand this tradeoff. Some may be as eager as the politicians to underpin the military effort with a sounder economic base.

Second, military as well as party figures have lately begun worrying about slack Soviet performance in technological innovation. Following extensive debate—and goaded by American rearmament and the lamentable showing of Soviet weaponry in the 1982 war in Lebanon—Leonid Brezhnev summed up the Soviet concern in one of his final public appearances, an unusual meeting with the entire military high command in the Kremlin. The struggle for supremacy in military technology, he said, had "sharply intensified" and was taking on "a fundamentally new character"; falling behind the West was "intolerable" for the Soviet Union.[43] A reformist political leadership would not have much difficulty persuading many officers that, without domestic changes, the USSR will continue to lose ground in the age of robotics, lasers, and computer microchips. Recognizing their growing dependence on innovation in the civilian sector, the generals can only be aware that improvements in the military-industrial complex alone will be futile.

A third point has to do with the army's other political interests. Along with being professional warriors, Soviet officers are also consumers and providers. Their coddled position has not been enough to insulate them fully from the effects of Soviet economic and social mismanagement. High military salaries produce frustration when there are insufficient decent goods to purchase. Lately, due to irregular deliveries of food at some military outlets, military buyers, like their civilian counterparts, "are being forced to become nervous and to waste valuable time waiting in queues." According to another report in the military press, underinvestment and poor personnel practices in the army's retailing network have bred bad service, spoiled goods, and "interruptions in supply," with hoarding and black markets as a consequence. All these "call forth justified indignation on the part of the residents of the garrisons."[44] Military families would thus gain as much from economic renewal as civilians, something they have better reason to appreciate today than in the past.

In sum, neither the KGB nor the military establishment is likely to block the movement toward moderate reform. Nor is there good evidence that either is becoming sufficiently powerful to decide the issue one way or the other. Instead, barring an upheaval in the political system as a whole, party relations with the military and KGB will remain a partnership, with the party the senior partner. As between the police and the army, the army is apt to play a greater role in key decisions. While it will doubtless seek to preserve its share of the economic pie, it well may join other political leaders in their efforts to enlarge the pie through reform.

4
Reform and the Soviet Future

The Improbability of Fundamental Change

As new leaders take charge during the next five to ten years, the Soviet Union stands at a fateful crossroads. After almost two decades on the same course, choices must now be made about the country's near future—choices among revolution, reform (of which there are radical, moderate, and minimal versions), conservatism, and reaction.[1] Let me begin with the most dramatic possibilities. To be frank, the rigidity and durability of the Soviet system as well as the elite's fear of drastic change make these highly unlikely.

Revolution: The collapse of the system. A Soviet dissident, Andrei Amalrik, once asked whether the Soviet system would survive until the Orwellian year 1984.[2] With that famous year upon us, the answer seems clear enough. Revolutionary cataclysm is prohibitively unlikely because the essential prerequisite for it—an overall crisis of the political system—does not exist. The regime has worries aplenty, but not so many that it will soon collapse beneath their weight. True, if economic and other troubles intensify, it may find itself in a more precarious position, forced to resort increasingly to naked repression to stay in power. This eventuality cannot be excluded, although it assumes the problems at their severest and leadership incompetence at its greatest. Even were the regime's support to be sapped to this degree, one has to realize that the mechanisms of control are so pervasive and durable that it could persist for some time on their strength alone.

There are only two plausible ways by which the regime's grip on the population might be shattered. One is through defeat in a major war, of the magnitude that dealt a death blow to Russia's tsarist regime in World War I. Barring the lunacy of nuclear war with the United States, this is a contingency against which the Soviet Union's giant military establishment adequately shields it. The other script for disaster would be a massive flareup of ethnic conflict, an equally unlikely development. The nationality problem, while a serious and perhaps fatal challenge in the long run, ought to be containable well into the twenty-first century, when the consequences of the demographic surge of the Central Asians will make themselves felt. Where it will carry the Soviet system is for politicians several generations hence to anguish over.

Radical reform: Transformation from within. Next to revolution, radical reform—basic change of the Soviet system but by peaceful and more gradual means—would be the most audacious course. Radical reform is distinguished from the less sweeping varieties of reform by its concentration on the fundamentals of institutions and ideology. In the Soviet context, it could be expected to bring liberalization and a quotient of democratization. Without necessarily duplicating a Western system, it would extend citizens' liberties, multiply their opportunities for political participation, and make the state more directly responsible to them. A radical switch away from one-party dictatorship could come about in one of two main ways: from above, at the behest of the regime; or from below, under pressure from society.

The best example of radical reform from above in a Soviet-type system is Czechoslovakia's "Prague Spring" of 1968. Although the officials and intellectuals who initiated it and rallied public support for it wanted to cure a miscellany of economic and other ills, their imaginations were kindled primarily by an ethical and political vision.[3] Their "socialism with a human face," with a competitive political process and greater civil rights, was inspired by Czechoslovakia's democratic and constitutional heritage and by revolutionary ideals carried over from the party's days in opposition, only two decades earlier. Their dream, of course, ended in the occupation by Warsaw Pact troops in August 1968 (one of the masterminds of which was Yuri Andropov).

The chance of a "Moscow Spring" today is nil. Russia's democratic tradition remains too weak, and the effervescent politics of its Revolution is now too remote to have much effect. The regime's mistrust of the population and dedication to perpetuating its vanguard role, if necessary by coercive means, are far greater than was the case in Czechoslovakia. The danger of destabilization due to the USSR's ethnic diversity adds disincentive: new political freedoms would in all probability precipitate open demands by spokesmen for many non-Russian communities for home rule and even secession. Some controls can be modified, yet no present or foreseeable Soviet leader will tamper with the basic authoritarian credo of Leninism. Soviet theorists stoutly reject any dilution of either the "leading role of the party" (the party's control over politics) or "democratic centralism" (the leadership's control over the party). Do-gooders in Eastern Europe or the non-ruling parties may espouse institutionalized "pluralism" in society and the party, the Soviets say, but (in Chernenko's words) "practice shows that where 'pluralism' flourishes it leads only to the loss of the party's fighting efficiency, to the erosion of its ideological foundations and class boundaries, in a word to the conversion of the party into some kind of motley conglomeration of ideologically disconnected groups and groupings."[4] If would-be Alexander Dubčeks lurk in the upper or middle reaches of the Soviet Communist Party, they are doing a superb job of keeping their convictions to themselves.

The second brand of radical reform, from the grass roots up, was to be found in communist Poland in 1980–81. Here an independent trade union movement sprang into being and with other social forces unseated two party leaders, pried astonishing concessions from the regime, and eventually prompted General Jaruzelski's rearguard coup. Could this happen in the Soviet Union? Insofar as the Polish uprising was "a classic case of protest produced by disappointed rising expectations," there is a temptation to see some parallel, for regime performance and public expectations have also been diverging in the USSR.[5] The rash of spontaneous work stoppages at Soviet factories in the late 1970s and early 1980s (the 1980 walkouts at the Togliatti and Gorky automotive plants being the biggest ones) evoke thoughts of Poland. There have even been several attempts to found autonomous Soviet trade unions. Moreover, the virulence with which the Soviet leadership anathematized Solidarity, and the attention it has paid the anti-Solidarity theme in domestic propaganda, probably reflect some degree of apprehension.

With this the resemblance between the two countries ends. Solidarity's birth at the Gdansk shipyards occurred during the fourth spasm of mass blue-collar protest in Poland in twenty-five years. It came on the heels of a decade of egregious mishandling of the economy that stoked aspirations without delivering the promised rise in living standards. Its victim was a regime that, having been installed by foreign bayonets, had at no time earned more than the weakest legitimacy. Equally to the point, the Polish revolution, never having sunk deep roots, left important areas outside state and party domination, among them the Roman Catholic church, a free-thinking and Western-oriented intelligentsia, and a large private sector in agriculture. Elements of each contributed greatly to Solidarity's sixteen months of glory.

The Soviet system, by way of contrast, is twice as old and far more fully consolidated than its Polish counterpart. It was forged in a much more thorough and more violent revolution, which left far fewer pockets of autonomy. The regime is home grown and able to tap national pride, especially among Russians, in the country's economic advance and rise to superpower rank. It is no surprise that the wildcat strikes of the last half-decade were easily crushed, like all those before them, and that the fledgling free unions, with never more than several hundred active supporters, were swiftly eradicated by the KGB. Faithful to Russian tradition and in contrast to Poland, relations between worker activists and dissident intellectuals have been plagued by mutual mistrust. The Soviet Union has not yet faced even dress rehearsals comparable to the Polish riots of 1956, 1970, and 1976.

In short, the stumbling blocks to radical reform from below are very high. Soviet industrial workers remain the group that the regime will eye most nervously, but they lack the opportunity, traditions, intense grievances, and allies pushing them to mount a serious challenge. Although outbreaks of labor unrest may become more common in future, especially if economic welfare declines, "the structure of Soviet society will limit their impact."[6] Poles are said to have a tradition of believing in miracles; Russians do not.

Reaction: Back to Stalinism. Some observers—including a fair number of emigrés from the USSR—have forecast radical movement in the reverse direction, back to a more coercive and closed politics. They have in mind many of the features associated with the acme of Joseph Stalin's rule: leader worship; rampant insecurity for office-holders; hypercentralized, secretive, and doctrinaire decision making; strict abridgment of the population's freedoms, including its present right to select employment voluntarily; mass police terror and periodic purges of real or fancied enemies of the state; priority in the economy for investment and military spending over consumption; and Russocentric xenophobia toward foreigners and countries outside the Soviet camp.

Reactionary and neo-Stalinist trends undoubtedly were in play, along with others, in Brezhnev's Soviet Union. Even an avowedly reformist regime at the present juncture is apt to make selective use of repressive methods. Wholesale re-Stalinization, however, is something else. The odds are stacked tall against it.

Soviet Russia on the eve of Stalin's seizure of absolute power lay prone to the fate that befell it. Mass illiteracy and semi-literacy, millions of people set adrift by revolution, civil war and economic dislocation, a relative isolation from the world at large, a small and unrepresentative ruling party only recently escaped from conspiratorial politics and wedded to an untried ideology with a strong messianic streak, a prevalent identification of the state with the Russian nation—all left it vulnerable to Stalin's assault. Stalinism both completed the smashing of the old social bonds and cemented new ties between citizens and an overpowering central authority.[7] Now, a half-century later (and three decades after de-Stalinization), the Soviet Union is a very different place. It has near-universal literacy, is reasonably settled in its ways and mores, and is far less divorced from world developments and opinion. With its larger and more assertive non-Russian communities, Soviet society would be much more resistant today to the extreme Russian nationalism embraced by Stalin. The party is ten times larger than in 1930, has evolved a blandly managerial ethos, and is all but devoid of ideological fervor. It has recanted Stalin's murderous thesis about the "intensification of the class struggle," said to accompany the building of socialism and to justify the annihilation of all opposition. As Andropov said in a ringing reiteration of the post-Stalin position shortly before becoming General Secretary, the party accepts "the existence in society of diverse, non-identical points of view and interests" and deems that "the failure of the interests of various social groups to coincide does not end in antagonism."[8]

Could the unique social and cultural chemistry that made Stalinism possible be recreated from above? Could a zealous and flint-hearted strongman—perhaps someone, like Andropov, with experience in the KGB—retrace Stalin's steps despite differing conditions? Although the possibility should not be ruled out, it is extremely unlikely. The obstacles today are much greater than in Stalin's time. Thanks to him, Soviet politicians now comprehend what full-blown Stalinism is like. When Soviet leaders claim to have "extracted the necessary lessons from this difficult historical experience" (the words again are Andropov's), they are speaking volumes.[9] Some, perhaps many, members of the political class may long for a strong father figure in the Kremlin and even certain of Stalin's long-abandoned policies. But as a group they have no interest in returning to the nightmarish atmosphere of the Stalin era, to the dread of extinction, the anonymity, and the conformity so much their lot before 1953. It should not be overlooked that Nikita Khrushchev was thrown out for threatening the elite's preserve far less.

The economic and social content of the primal Stalinist model also loads the dice against re-Stalinization. Its genius was a ruthless use of state power to develop a primitive industrial economy. It is precisely the irrelevance of this old approach in a complex and demanding society that lies behind many current Soviet difficulties. To revive flagrantly coercive methods might shake free some economic reserves and yield one-time gains in productivity, but, as a sustainable strategy, the Stalinist gospel offers the Soviet Union no more than the nostrums of Herbert Hoover would the United States.[10]

The Realistic Alternatives

Conservatism and minimal reforms. If the Soviets avoid revolution, radical reform, and re-Stalinization, the choice for the near future is limited to a narrow range. One option widely predicted in the West is muddling through on essentially the post-1964 Brezhnev course. Preservation of existing institutions, beliefs, and policies would remain the party's arch objective. As under Brezhnev, reforms would be minimal and at the level of policy and technique, small adjustments causing a minimum of discord and inconvenience for vested interests.

Whoever sits around the Politburo table in the 1980s and 1990s, one can be sure, will want to safeguard the essence of the Soviet order—its Leninist ideology, its single-party system, and its state-owned economy. All well-anchored political systems rely on leaders and elites who remain committed to the system's basic features; but the Brezhnev leadership, especially in its later years, went well beyond this normal conservatism. Its excessive concern with stability produced increasing petrifaction, distorted priorities, and a failure to follow through on even minimal reforms.

The regime suffered from acute conservatism for several reasons. First, it was reacting deliberately to what it saw as the reformist excesses of the Khrushchev years. Second, Brezhnev, the man at the top, was colorless and unobtrusive in guiding the party, an ideological conservative who saw his role mainly in chairman-of-the-board terms (which is why his colleagues preferred him). Third, there was from the earliest days a power equilibrium within the inner leadership and between it and the wider governing stratum, creating a strong inhibition against serious changes in either personnel or policy. Fourth, top positions were filled by members of an aged generation lodged in high office for an abnormally long time. And fifth, Brezhnevism worked at the outset, making it harder to change when it ceased to work.

For the regime to preserve the style and approach of the Brezhnev years, these conditions will have to persist or some substitute be found, not a likely prospect. Changes are already in motion that make the conservative consensus of recent years increasingly unviable and improve the chances of moderate but genuine reform.

Moderate reform. Moderate reform refers to a strategy of controlled change somewhere between radical and minimal reform. Its focus would be on public policy and the machinery needed to fulfill change, not on basic institutions and beliefs. Hence it falls well short of radical reform. But, unlike minimal reform, the change involved will pose a challenge to some established groups and thereby generate controversy and conflict.

The problems now facing the regime seem likely to promote moderate reform over the other plausible course, conservatism with modest tinkering or, as it is sometimes captioned, Brezhnevism without Brezhnev. First, with Brezhnev gone, the way is clear for a reassessment of his legacy. If the soundest basis for predicting the course of political succession is "an analysis of the policy failures of the preceding regime," an opening to reform would now be natural and in tune with Soviet political history.[11] As Khrushchev's reforms were a reaction to Stalin's tyranny and Brezhnev's stabilizing program a counter to Khrushchev's erratic reformism, the new policies will likely attack the lethargy and sclerosis of the late Brezhnev era.

Second, the Soviet Union has now experienced the brief but bracing rule of Andropov, who saw himself as an activist and advocate of moderate reform. While evincing no interest in radical or reckless changes, he emphasized the importance of substantial improvements in the economy and in other areas and condemned "half-measures" such as were typical of Brezhnev. His interim successor, Chernenko, seems on early evidence to concur in most of Andropov's ideas. His Politburo is more likely to want Andropovism without Andropov than Brezhnevism without Brezhnev.

Third, deaths and retirements are altering the post-1964 political balance within the party hierarchy. Andropov revoked the implicit contract guaranteeing security of office and began to reshape the leadership. His early victories showed the new importance of sound policy in succession politics and the inadequacy of patronage alone. Chernenko's age and health make another leadership contest (and perhaps several) likely within several years, and that may lead to confusion and change, but candidates will probably have to espouse policies approximately resembling Andropov's to be credible contenders.

Fourth, a generation of leaders now in their forties and fifties and recruited into politics after Stalin's death is finally advancing into high positions. Their full arrival will not occur until the end of the 1980s, yet the effects are already being felt. Many of the new people are impatient with shopworn excuses and ready to try judicious innovations, especially in economic policy.

Fifth, the tally of Soviet economic and social difficulties has been lengthening steadily in recent years. Stale solutions are becoming noticeably less effective. Auguring well for moderate reform is the degree of the regime's problems—serious, but not yet bad enough to call its survival into question. As one scholar says of reform in general, "Perhaps the hardest lesson to learn for governments sensitive to the needs of reform is the importance of introducing reforms from a position of strength. Reforms which appear to be granted under pressure from events and the demands of more radical groups can only further weaken the regime, strengthen the radicals, lead to more extreme demands from more groups, and provoke a counter-revolutionary backlash."[12] A Soviet leadership as embattled as the Shah of Iran in the late 1970s or the Polish government in the early 1980s might be still readier to try temperate reform, but with less prospect of success. The longer the regime procrastinates, the more it fritters away the advantage of strength. A unique window of opportunity exists today for policy-centered reform. A decade ago, that window was not yet open because the problems of the Soviet system were not sufficiently severe; a decade hence, it may be closed by problems that have become too grave.

Five Points of Moderate Reform

Without being able to detail the content or timing of moderate reform, one can sketch its most likely features. The USSR's problems provide some guidance. So do the innumerable and increasingly candid discussions of particular remedies now under way in the Soviet Union. And so do the initial rhetoric and actions of the Andropov regime, which amount to a respectable beginning on a process of moderate internal reform and apparently will be extended in modified form under Chernenko. One can also learn from the record of reform in other communist countries, something Soviet officials are now being enjoined to do by their leaders.

The agenda for moderate reform in the Soviet Union involves mainly economic and socioeconomic issues, five in particular: law and order; private economic initiative; the apportionment of central resources; new incentives; and decentralization of industrial management.

Law and order. Yuri Andropov's opening step as leader was to issue a clarion call for "socialist discipline." Though long overdue, it did not come as an abrupt break with the past, and it had the added virtue of furnishing prompt if limited economic gains cheaply. "Putting things in order," Andropov remarked in early 1983, "really does not demand any capital investments at all, yet it has an enormous effect."[13]

The Andropov law-and-order offensive directed its fire broadly, by means of increased police checks in the baths and movie theaters, volunteer street patrols, and squads of party members mobilized against loiterers, alcoholics, wife-beaters, ticketless streetcar riders, and urban dwellers without residence permits. Soon, however, the campaign concentrated on two areas. The first was the work place, where lazy employees, drunkards, and truants were bullied and exhorted to shape up. An August 1983 decree put teeth into the campaign by authorizing managers to reduce the vacations of persons who miss work or drink at their stations, dock their pay, and even fire them without first consulting the factory trade union commit-tee.[14] The attempt to revive the work ethic smacks in limited ways of the authoritarian management practices of the Stalinist past, but it is hard to see how any program of economic revitalization could do without it.

The second thrust of the drive has been against corruption, a blight that spread in the 1960s and 1970s and that, as other societies have learned, would sooner or later have devastating effects on the system as a whole if unchecked. Unprecedented press coverage of venality in public office has been accompanied by the sacking of two Central Committee members (Nikolai Shchelokov, the long-time head of the Ministry of the Interior, and Sergei Medunov, once the party prefect in the Krasnodar resort region) and the announced investigation for malfeasance of a former chief of the trade unions, Aleksei Shibayev. There have been rapid promotions of of-ficials known to take a stringent line against corruption, such as Vitali Vorotnikov, the new chairman of the Russian Republic government (pre-viously Medunov's replacement in Krasnodar) and Geidar Aliyev of Azer-baidzhan, the new second-in-command of the Council of Ministers (who in his home republic in the 1970s forbade senior officials to build dachas or buy personal automobiles). Under Shchelokov's replacement, Vitali Fedorchuk, the barrel-chested KGB stalwart who had been Andropov's suc-cessor as KGB chief in May 1982, the ranks of the uniformed police "are being purged of unworthy people who are ideologically and morally im-mature," and new party organs have been established in the ministry.[15] More energetic action against influence peddling by the police and others has been reported, including death sentences and execution for some offenders. Shchelokov's first deputy, Yuri Churbanov — the husband of Leonid Brezh-nev's daughter Galina — has been demoted to a provincial post, and word was circulating in Moscow in 1983 of upcoming trials that would tie Brezh-nev's relatives and confidants to wrongdoing. Accounts of local party con-ferences in early 1984 stated that hundreds of party members and func-tionaries had been expelled from the party for moral transgressions.[16]

Chernenko, with his intimate association with Brezhnev, may well want to suppress suggestions that Brezhnev and his coterie were personally re-sponsible for the growth of corruption and to rule out legal proceedings against his family. Beyond that, Chernenko has shown no inclination to cut the drive short, and he probably would be taking a large political risk if he did so. "The party and state," he said in March 1984, "have stepped up the struggle against such shameful phenomena as squandering of state resources, deceit, abuse of official position, embezzlement, and bribery. This is not a temporary campaign. It is a line that will be carried out stead-ily and strictly. Here there is not and will not be any leniency. No one should harbor any illusions on this account."[17]

Reducing corruption in the bureaucracy, it must be said, will not be as difficult as deciding how to deal with the small fry in the underground economy: the moonlighters, itinerant fruit and vegetable vendors, sticky-fingered salesclerks, and the like who, inhabiting a limbo between legality and illegality, have increasingly found customers for goods and services that the state cannot or will not supply. Although the leaders do not want to see the second economy grow further, most also seem to accept it as a buffer performing politically and economically useful functions. Destroying it is at present neither practical nor, for most in the regime, desirable. Better and more consistent policing is called for; but doing only this, without addressing the economic failures causing the problem, is certain to fall short and to breed further disenchantment.

Private enterprise. One way to realize quick economic gains at little cost is to give greater license to private producers. The precedent is the household plots allowed Soviet peasants since the 1930s, which occupy only about 4 percent of arable land but produce 60 percent of the country's potatoes, over 40 percent of its eggs and fruit, and about 30 percent of its meat, milk, and vegetables. Brezhnev, already more lenient than his predecessors, upgraded the private plots in 1977 and 1981 legislation. Some city residents have also been given patches of land to cultivate, and their produce is now making its way into the legal urban markets.

The post-Brezhnev line on the household plots has been generally positive, although little concrete has been done—most likely because of indifference on Andropov's and Chernenko's part. (A younger leader like Gorbachev might be more forthcoming.) If private food production is to be stimulated, the carping of ideological purists will have to be silenced. Reformist economists point to some of the countries of Eastern Europe where personal plots, located on state-owned land and dependent on government supplies, are a bona fide part of "socialist agriculture." But merely adjusting doctrine will not suffice. Capital and equipment will also have to be made available to the private producer. For the record, the discussion in the press incorporates a great many ideas, such as guaranteed access to state feed (without which private tending of livestock is declining), the extension of credit, the provision of seed, fertilizer, and, most important, small machinery such as works marvels on miniature plots in Japan, help with storage and transport, a suburban garden as a retirement right for all city dwellers, and (least likely to be granted) the enlargement of the maximum plot size from the present 0.5 hectares (about 1.2 acres).

A cleaner break with past policy would have to be made to unshackle private initiative outside of agriculture. But, if anything, the return in output and good will would be greater here. Talk of the value of private activity in consumer-related fields—sometimes camouflaged as family, "cooperative," or "brigade" production, with East European practice in mind—has been allowed in the USSR since the mid-1970s, and lately it has increased. The most prevalent suggestions are for individuals and small firms, subject to inspection and taxation, to build and maintain housing, operate taxicabs and delivery trucks, repair appliances and clothing, provide other household services, and sell prepared foods. Since illegal activity has burgeoned in all these areas, the regime could turn much of this to its ends while reducing the underground economy. The natural step, as many advocates shrewdly point out, would be to combine approval for some private activity with a clampdown on black market profiteers in other fields.

Reallocating resources. Soviet politicians during the first two post-Stalin successions have made at least temporary budgetary concessions to consumers. The post-Brezhnev leadership has been expressing similar solicitude, stressing, as Andropov observed in 1983, that shortages and poor quality "bring about . . . dissatisfaction among the people." While black markets must be curbed by punitive means, he said, "the main thing is that we must steadily increase the production and improve the quality of goods and intensively develop the service sphere, in order to liquidate completely shortages of goods and services."[18] Changed circumstances, however, make it harder for the leadership to succeed. Resources are now at a premium, and the population, jaded by earlier broken promises, will be unimpressed by platitudes.

The regime is already trying to link consumer benefits more closely with productivity, as will be explored in a moment. The improvement thus is likely to be directed at more specific groups of consumers (those whose productivity is high), but for the same reason may also be more substantial and lasting than in the past. Local party officials and economists have for some time been clamoring for reversal of Brezhnev's spending cuts on housing and "public consumption" (schools, health, recreation, and municipal utilities), on the grounds that a substandard living environment grinds down worker motivation. Now, if a Central Committee resolution made in February 1983 is to be believed, the leadership is set to move on this point, particularly on housing. Other joint party-government resolutions in March and May 1983 called for the opening of more cleaning and repair shops, more personal services such as hairdressing and film developing, easier rental of consumer durables, more convenient working hours in service establishments, and an immediate "substantial increase" in the output of consumer products, including the small household items and spare parts in such acutely short supply.[19]

Unavoidably, the leadership has come flush up against the problem of coordinating the chaotic consumer sector where, as one expert remarks, "No hortatory style of leadership, good wishes, directives, or paper threats are going to have an effect."[20] Just how the regime will proceed is uncertain, but in late 1983 a special Politburo commission, chaired by Aliyev, began meeting to draft an "integrated program" for developing consumer goods production and services. It has already been decided that heavy industry will be given more detailed instructions on consumer production in the 1986–90 five-year plan. Local governments and party organs are being urged to intervene more forcefully on the consumer's behalf and promised greater powers in doing so, and in December 1983 the time of one national party secretary (Ivan Kapitonov) was allocated fully to light industry. In early 1984 it was announced that an experiment in improving material incentives for service firms would be started in eight regions of the Russian Republic in July 1984.[21]

Unfortunately for the regime, the decline in economic growth and the still faster drop in capital spending mean that it will have great difficulty maintaining investment, let alone increasing it, while doing better by the consumer. Inadequate investment means a future slackening of economic growth. So where will Moscow find the investment funds needed for updating such economic dinosaurs as Soviet metallurgy, construction, and rail transport? The fattest target for cuts is the defense budget, yet the extravagant expenditures on energy development, distorting terribly the whole investment effort of the last five years, may also be reconsidered. Criticisms of waste in the Siberian oil and gas fields became more pointed in 1983, and energy conservation is being debated seriously for the first time; in December 1982 the Supreme Soviet set up standing committees on energy, a decision recommended personally by Andropov. A third enticing source of capital is the prodigal agriculture budget, which, apart from its untold sums for investment, much of it squandered on irrigation and land reclamation boondoggles, also includes food price subsidies totalling over 50 billion rubles in 1983. The May 1982 "food program," the last big decision steered through the Central Committee by Brezhnev, was a bid to fix and expand these spending commitments. Although the broad terms of the new program have been affirmed by Andropov and Chernenko, it will be odd if the new leaders do not scale down spending, particularly if better work incentives and private enterprise yield results and Western grain continues to be available at markdown prices.

New work incentives.   Some of Andropov's most scathing remarks dealt with the need for incentives to stimulate efficient and high-quality labor and "enterprise" among the labor force. While punishing loafers is part of the answer, so are several affirmative actions long discussed by Soviet specialists and now finding a growing audience among officials. The most significant of these is revamping of the egalitarian earnings structure in effect since the mid-1950s and little modified under Brezhnev. In Andropov's view, once Soviet citizens receive life's bare necessities, each "has the right to only those material goods that correspond to the quantity and quality of his socially useful labor."[22] He meant that only people who work harder than average or perform more irreplaceable services should receive bigger pay envelopes, other tangible returns, and promotions. This theme has been taken up by Chernenko, who has stated that "whoever gives his all in his work absolutely must get preference in pay" and that "punishment by the ruble" of inefficient workers must become more severe.[23]

Accordingly, the state wage bureaucracy (under a new chief, Yuri Batalin) is laying the groundwork for slower rates of general wage increase and for wider pay disparities. The August 1983 directive on labor discipline also instructed managers to start giving preference on waiting lists for flats and vacation passes to industrious employees. Andropov endorsed the expansion of cooperative ownership of housing, including housing for the aged, and making space there available to the most productive workers, while Chernenko has made reference to greater opportunities in future for private housing construction. Others are talking of pegging rents and apartment sizes in state buildings to productivity.

The post-Brezhnev Politburo has also shown new interest in the "brigade" or small-group method of organizing labor and compensation, long extolled in the abstract but not put into practice. In agriculture, the leaders, especially Mikhail Gorbachev, have actively promoted a complicated variant called the "collective contract system," which rewards teams of farm workers according to the size of their deliveries of produce. In industry, decrees by the party, government, and trade union federation in December 1983 ordered the overcoming of ministerial resistance to brigade organization and for the first time specified the bonuses to be paid brigade leaders. The party resolution on the industrial brigades, setting no deadlines and saying the brigades should be created "without excessive haste," obviously will have to be followed up vigorously if anything is to come of it.[24]

The Kremlin may in addition substantially revise consumer prices— not a reform in itself, but definitely an innovation if, as has been hinted, it relates prices to availability. The regime has sharply criticized the long-standing practice of freezing the prices of important consumer goods while allowing wages, nominal purchasing power, and expectations to soar. In early 1983 steep price increases were levied on some consumer products and most construction materials, and Andropov spoke (as Brezhnev never did) of the need to iron out "distortions and discrepancies" throughout the price structure.[25] An inconclusive discussion of price formation has continued since then. If instituted, an altered price system could have prodigious implications, particularly if it eases the way for fuller acceptance of prices and markets as mechanisms of distribution and control. It would free some of the resources tied down in large subsidies (meat prices, for example, remain at their 1962 levels) and presumably would sop up excess demand and shorten the queues at state stores. It may help to curtail underground economy activities spurred by the discrepancy between official and black market prices, which now invites warehouse and retailing employees to pull merchandise off the shelves, sell it on the side for the going price, and pocket the difference. It could also give a shot in the arm to the legal private sector, if this were sought by the regime, by enabling legitimate entrepreneurs to get materials and supplies from state outlets, rather than by today's common ruses of pilfering and under-the-table arrangements.

Industrial decentralization.   The most contentious item on the reform agenda, and the most problematic in the execution, is the reorganization of industry, the chief generator of national wealth. Most of the senior generation of Soviet leaders would be satisfied with some tidying up of central planning (partly through better use of computers), new Manhattan Project-type campaigns for the latest priorities, moving of personnel and techniques from the military-industrial complex into civilian industry, and the usual reshuffling of the boxes on the organization chart. Yet, there are those in the establishment, especially among younger officials and economists, who would like to try a fresh approach.

For many of these individuals, the way forward has been illuminated by the USSR's small client state, Hungary. Hungary's so-called New Economic Mechanism, put in place in 1968 by leader János Kádár, sought basically to overcome the numbing overcentralization of the command economy.[26] It replaced obligatory physical plans and central interference in the firm—the crude "thumbs" of the classic Soviet model—with the "fingers" of indirect, decentralized controls. Although Hungarian factories remained the property of the state, their relations with one another and with planners were now mediated in large part by the market. It was a highly regulated market, but a market all the same, with autonomous buyers and sellers arriving at agreements on the basis of price. Plant directors were far more independent than before, and profit maximization, tied to bonuses and other employee incentives, served as the main operational goal. Rewards were given for developing new products and conserving capital, labor, and materials.

Will the Soviet Union imitate Hungary? The only thing that is clear is that this question, closed under Brezhnev, was reopened by Yuri Andropov, a former ambassador to Hungary and the top Soviet authority on Eastern Europe when the Kádár reforms were being hammered out. Ten days after being appointed General Secretary, he publicly indicated a definite interest in exploring decentralization of some form: "Recently not a little has been said about the need to expand the independence of associations [industrial trusts] and enterprises, collective and state farms. I think the time has come to get down to a practical decision on this question." He added that experiments are necessary and that stock should be taken of reforms in the Soviet bloc (Hungary was not mentioned by name), and also that decentralization "must in all cases be combined with greater accountability and with concern for national interests." In later statements, Andropov returned to the decentralization question, pressing for the wider use of "economic levers and stimuli," including prices, credit, and ample rewards for innovation.[27]

In late 1982 a working group headed by a new Central Committee secretary, Nikolai Ryzhkov—relatively young (born in 1929) and the former director of the largest factory in the Soviet Union, the Ural Machine-Building works in Sverdlovsk—set about developing proposals for streamlining planning and management. The intramural debate has been heated, occasionally boiling over into the press. As one confidential memorandum making the rounds in Moscow in 1983 said, the issue is intensely political, since any overhaul big enough to stir industry from its doldrums "cannot but produce conflict." Progress, the memorandum (by pro-reform economists from Novosibirsk) maintained, would be possible only "on the basis of a well-thought-out strategy aimed at galvanizing those groups that are interested in the change and immobilizing those groups that might hamper it." The battle lines are complex. Opposition joins the industrial ministries to the "less qualified and more inert" personnel at the plant level, especially from the older age group. Gosplan, the powerful planning headquarters—whose chief since 1965, Nikolai Baibakov, remains in office and is openly cool toward decentralization—is split on the problem.[28]

The first concrete decision, a joint party-government resolution promulgated July 26, 1983, reflects a standoff, setting the stage for additional debate.[29] Beginning January 1, 1984, a major experiment is being conducted in five industrial ministries, two of them at the national level (one of them manufacturing both heavy machinery for civilian use and tanks for the army) and three in the republics. Managers in these industries have unusual leeway to decide on output, operations, and disposal of profits—and even, under certain conditions, on the prices of new products—and will be judged by the marketability of their goods instead of the old physical plan indicators. Unlike both the half hearted general reform of 1965 and the isolated management experiments of the late Brezhnev era, this scheme is designed to be highly visible and has the enthusiastic patronage of top politicians.

The timetable for further change is unsettled. Andropov said after the experiment was announced that he wanted the economy "fully armed" by January 1986, the shoving-off point of the next five-year plan, but it was unclear whether he intended the reorganization of industry to be completed by that date, or merely that further experiments be started up by then, or that preliminary agreement on broad management principles be reached. Chernenko's statements have been no more revealing on the timing question, though they are virtually indistinguishable from Andropov's on the desirability of shifting some major economic decisions away from central planners and sharply increasing the independence of plant-level management. Whatever his wishes, the regime—more than likely under another new leader—will within several years face the question of whether to extend decentralization to the economy at large.

For several reasons, all underlaid by Soviet conservatism and concern over the erosion of power at the center—reasons which, as I shall indicate shortly, should not be overdrawn—thorough decentralization along Hungarian lines will probably not come about immediately. First, the Soviets are well aware that Kádár's formula has not been an economic cure-all. Old habits have lingered tenaciously, Hungarian growth has been disappointing to some, and the reform has gone through a number of course corrections, most recently in 1980. Second, marketization requires a larger leap into the unknown than other reform projects. For it to work, it cannot be done halfway. In Poland, where Edward Gierek's regime tried to mimic Hungary while leaving intact much of the old, top-heavy apparatus, "the result of following such a policy was the gradual suffocation of the new system," creating the economic fiasco of the late 1970s.[30] Third, as Soviet conservatives point out, the Soviet economy is dissimilar in structure to that of Hungary. Decentralization, they say, would be much harder to achieve and control in a country of 270 million people (to Hungary's 10 million), sprawled over eleven time zones and with economic priorities that include provisioning and arming a huge military establishment.

Still, when Western specialists recite these arguments, they tend to underplay the strong counterarguments made publicly and privately by Soviet proponents of some variant of market socialism. Those who make the other thesis stress that Hungary's restructuring, while admittedly no magic answer, has produced results overwhelmingly popular among the Hungarian people and exciting to the thousands of visiting Soviets (who load up their shopping bags in the shops of Budapest). Second, the Soviets have learned from the Polish debacle, as well as from their own lack of success with partial decentralization. Indeed, the failure of the 1965 Soviet reform, given too little room to work, rather resembles earlier experiences that led the Hungarians to embrace a deeper reform. Third, the very bigness of the Soviet economy also makes it in some ways better suited to controlled marketization. The transition to decentralized operations might be bumpier, but overcentralization is also less workable in the vast Soviet Union than it was in Hungary before 1968.

How, then, will the issue eventually be resolved? Much will depend on the results of less ambitious economic reforms in the areas of discipline, private enterprise, budgets, and work incentives. If the improved economic results of 1983 are followed by other good years—as must seriously be doubted, should no further changes be made—the leadership may conclude that no structural reform of industry is required. In the Soviet context, a literal copying of the New Economic Mechanism is bound to be considered by some tantamount to radical rather than moderate reform, and conservatives will try to exploit this perception. They will likewise insist, probably with some success, that even if microeconomic planning (direct central intervention in the firm) is reduced, macroeconomic planning (setting the economy's general direction and proportions) must remain firm and grow in sophistication.[31] Many conservatives will also prefer to dawdle with the implementation of decentralization and to do further experiments, which they can then bog down in red tape.

If the safest bet is that conservatives will prevail over the next few years, it is not a foregone conclusion that time is on their side. Indefinite delay will, as I see it, put the defects of the inherited system into more vivid relief, and it will allow younger and less hidebound politicians to reach peak office. The atmosphere of economic experimentation, and the Politburo's apparent resolve to have the structural issue thoroughly debated, will help the partisans of change. Reformers will have to tailor their schemes to Soviet realities, and especially to the "concern for national interests" to which Andropov referred. If they do so, as the 1980s wear on, the advantage well may swing to them.

The Strategy and Politics of Moderate Reform

In our culture's idealized image, the political reformer is a person of box-office qualities—a spellbinding orator, an enemy of injustice, a champion of society's victims. In the real world, he is more likely to be a man with a dilemma than a man with a cause. The reformer usually is undecided on how far to push change and leery of damaging institutions in which he believes. Typically, he is the last person to shout his ideas from a soapbox. "It is of the essence of the reformer," Samuel Huntington reminds us, "that he must employ ambiguity, concealment, and deception concerning his goals."[32] He must be as nimble at disarming conservatives as at pleasing those in his own camp. Rarely does he provoke a single, climactic battle against the foe. Instead, to quote a landmark study of the subject, the reformer must pull off "extraordinary feats of contriving" in the course of which some hostile groups are won over, others are outsmarted, and the die-hards are "barely overcome by a coalition of highly heterogeneous forces."[33]

Moderate reform in the Soviet Union, if that is indeed what lies ahead, will obey the same dialectic, adjusted to peculiar Soviet circumstances. Its proponents will have to cover their right flank by placating conservatives and reactionaries: soothing their fears, buying them off with concessions and side payments, and confusing them over the ultimate destination of reform. Moderate reformers in the USSR, moreover, will not want to reform everything. The current movement is selective and discernible only on economic and socioeconomic issues. In other areas, the Soviet elite is either conservative—not wanting, as Andropov said in 1983, to lose "a single valuable grain" of cherished experience—or, on occasion, thoroughly reactionary. In the field of civil and intellectual freedoms, for example, where a radical reformer would demand liberalization, most moderate Soviet reformers will not. If anything, the trend since November 1982 is toward harsher cultural policies: a further stifling of dissent, shriller demands for "vigilance" against foreign ideas, more regimentation for the arts, a near-cessation of Jewish emigration, more Russian-language classes for the minorities.

The emerging strategy of moderate reform will, consequently, be as much a blend as was the predominantly conservative approach of the Brezhnev years. It will mingle reformism, conservatism, and reaction. There will be more of the first element, but nothing like a disappearance of the other two and no rupture with past policies.

Moderate reform will be clouded in several other respects. For one, after several decades in which sundry reform proposals and minor experiments have been floated, less effort is apt to go into inventing novel solutions than into implementing familiar ones. Many ideas have been around for a long time, such as inducements for technological breakthroughs, help for the private plots, greater housing and services budgets for local governments, penalties for drinking on the job, the brigade system, and even decentralization of industry. All these date back to Khrushchev's period, all were endorsed to some degree by the Brezhnev administration, but almost none has been seriously pursued. Reform stands to be ambiguous, too, because modern reformers may see as one of their missions the reversal of some earlier reforms. Wages and labor discipline are cases in point. Thirty years ago it was considered a forward-looking step to mitigate the extreme inequality of earnings and the quasi-military factory discipline bequeathed by Stalin; today, wage leveling and worker indiscipline have long since been a brake on economic growth.

Moderate reform may also lack a certain clarity because its advocates do not have master plans. Soviet politics, in the absence of competitive elections and periodic mass insurrections, does not generate grand visions for change. With the agony of earlier revolutions imposed from above still fresh in their minds, many Soviet reformers have made plain the harmfulness of all-inclusive plans: "After all, we are not talking here [on improving Soviet life] of a designer's studio, but about a historical process, during which the forms of our life take shape under the influence of a multitude of subjective and objective factors impossible of precise measurement. Consequently, the ambitious intent to create a detailed blueprint and construct according to it an ideal way of life is doomed to failure."[34]

Andropov's confession that he had no "readymade recipes" is fully in accord with this position, and it should be taken at face value. Hence a program of moderate reform under his successors will surely be eclectic and slow to unfold. It will have to be often reaffirmed and refitted in the long process of implementation; it will also have to be periodically rescued from its errors and conceits.

Its most important contradiction will be between ends and means. This is the moderate reformer's worst dilemma: without a radical change in the political system, which he does not want, he is compelled often *to use unreformed, largely authoritarian methods* in pursuit of his goals. Moderate reform in its Soviet incarnation may bring a loosening of some constraints on individual behavior—for instance, on the private provision of services or on factory directors' use of their prerogatives—but no comprehensive relaxation or liberalization is in the offing. When necessary, stern and at times draconian measures will be applied to push reform forward and keep social friction from degenerating into open strife.

As a consequence, Soviet leaders will continue to assign a strong role to central instruments of control, among them the party, the KGB, and censorship, and may in some ways want to strengthen those instruments further. Any administrative decentralization will focus on getting the economic apparatus to work better, perforce to work harder. Where low-level officials prefer the old and tried ways, the pro-reform forces will want, as one commentator on the five-ministry experiment stated in November 1983, "to seriously reeducate such executives, to force them to think creatively and display initiative."[35] Where technological obsolescence and overmanning are the problem, the regime will feel the need for stiff rules to control the evasions of middle and lower management. In defense-related industry, where no letdown in the competition with the West can be expected, it will wish to monitor performance more closely. It is one of the ironies of the situation that in the Soviet Union decentralization itself will require careful prodding from the center. As one Soviet commentator notes, in a bureaucratic milieu in which centralization is as natural as gravity, decentralizing impulses have no chance without "constant, purposive regulation on the part of the state."[36]

Like prudent reformers everywhere, Soviet reformers must guard against a ballooning of popular expectations. In Hungary, the lid was kept on by memories of the repression following the 1956 revolution and by the shadow of a watchful Soviet Union. Poland imposed no limit and, in fact, borrowed heavily abroad to begin a revolution of rising expectations that could not be satisfied. Reform-minded Soviet politicians clearly intend to avoid this trap. Whether by puritanical sermons and calls for sacrifice or by coercion and minimizing foreign contacts, they will do their utmost to prevent popular aspirations from outstripping the likely returns from reform.

Social inequalities constitute a further source of trouble. They will grow sharper if private enterprise is expanded and the Soviet incentive structure reformed, and this risks engendering resentment among those whose incomes will be hit hardest. In Poland, the introduction of merit-based pay "made sense in purely economic terms . . . [but] challenged the prevalent ethos of egalitarianism." Many in Solidarity nursed grievances over such perceived injustices.[37] In Hungary, the fear of worker reaction convinced the government to water down plans for stratifying earnings. The attitude of most workers in the Soviet Union would be no different, at least initially. Arguably, however, the Soviet leadership is in a better position than its East European confederates simply to ramrod through a change in incentive policy.

Much as reformers are able to defend them on rational grounds, other of the foreseeable moves in the quest for economic productivity and efficiency—pricing consumer products to reflect scarcity, expansion of managers' rights, greater enterprise autonomy—promise to be equally unpopular with specific segments of the population. Consumers will be afraid of the unaffordability of goods, wage earners of the confiscation of savings, and workers of the loss of jobs: even members of these groups who accept reform in principle will want to limit its applicability to their own case. Far-reaching industrial decentralization, the most extreme tactic under consideration, would be the most disruptive, particularly if it led to large-scale plant closings and mounting unemployment (which it might if profit were made the main criterion of survival). Some of the worst shocks can be cushioned (by, for example, wage increases to offset higher food prices), but there will nonetheless be insecurity, inconveniences, and costs for many social groups before the putative benefits begin to flow. That the market or some local power center may do the collecting will not make the costs less onerous. Again, there are lessons for the Soviets in Eastern Europe. Squeamishness about raising Polish workers' food prices hamstrung Gierek's reforms, and in Hungary anxiety over a social explosion if too much were done too soon diminished the effect of the 1968 reform. "It is the alliance of conservative forces [in the bureaucracy] with the populace," one American economist rightly observes about Hungary, " . . . which represents a truly formidable threat to the reformers."[38] In the Soviet Union, such an alliance would be no less a menace to the reform coalition. Reformers may plan that eventually education and success will sell the changes, but in the short run they may be tempted to use stronger-arm methods.

In the final analysis, moderate reform in the Soviet Union will stand or fall on the political skill of the reformers. "The reform leader," as Huntington says, must be able "to inspire confidence and provide some measure of charismatic leadership, while at the same time having the political ability and adaptability to engage in log-rolling and back-scratching, to shift allies and enemies from one issue to the next, to convey different messages to different audiences, to sense the eddies and tides of public opinion and time his actions accordingly, and to hide his ultimate purpose behind his immediate rhetoric."[39] The Soviet reformer must do all this while maintaining precarious balances. He must lead and lean on officials and the public, but without trampling on them or alienating them to the point he loses their cooperation. He must be responsive without seeming weak-kneed, flexible but not directionless. He must use central power to promote decentalization and a gargantuan state to stimulate individual initiative.

Moderate reform, in keeping with its purpose, would not transform Soviet society or revolutionize political institutions and ideology. It would, however, put a perceptible dent in the Soviet Union's problems, which is all that most of its backers expect of it. Properly executed, it would counteract negative economic and social trends that worry the population and the regime alike. Its makers could reduce corruption and improve the quality and availability of consumer goods and services. They could realistically hope to add several percentage points to annual economic performance — not a spectacular result, but enough to reverse the decline in growth rates, resume the gradual improvement in living standards and the equally slow closing of the economic gap with the West, and increase the sum available for dealing with social problems such as the deterioration of the health care system. They could hope also to stem the unfavorable drift in popular attitudes, and especially the belief, which grew in the late Brezhnev period, that the regime cannot satisfy mass aspirations and that individuals are best advised to seek fulfillment in private pursuits. If conservatives or reactionaries gain the upper hand in the 1980s, or if bungled reforms come to naught, none of these things will be achieved and pressing problems will go unrectified. The likelihood would then be high that the 1990s would bring a crisis of legitimacy and far more searching dilemmas for the regime, with its core structures and values open to question and under attack as never before.

5

The Changing Soviet Union and the World

Foreign and Domestic Policy in Interaction

Everywhere in the contemporary world, the interaction between foreign and domestic issues has widened and intensified. The causes are various: breakthroughs in communications and transportation technology, shrinking the distances between peoples and spilling information and controversy across state borders; the calculus of modern warfare and military deterrence, requiring the mobilization of the resources of society as a whole for the sake of defense; mutual vulnerability to global demographic and ecological problems; trends in the world economy, now earmarked by growing competition, technological borrowing, and interpenetration of national industry and finance. For the great powers, there is a supplementary and more expressly political logic: elected leaders and dictators, in addition to tending to domestic constituencies, are custodians of universalist ideologies that must be upheld abroad, and their performance in office is judged accordingly.

For decades, the Soviet regime denied much of this reality. Stalin's teaching of "socialism in one country" envisioned the USSR as self-sufficient in most essential respects—as a source of revolutionary enlightenment and energy for the world, but not actively engaged with it in many other ways. Since his death, the Soviet attitude has changed greatly. Yuri Andropov put the new consensus starkly while still in the KGB: "We do not live behind a fence shutting us off from the external world. The internal development of the Soviet Union is closely tied to the state of affairs in the world arena. We must take precise account of what happens there in drawing up our plans and defining the articles of expenditure in our budget. By the same token, the achievements of the Soviet Union . . . now exert a powerful influence on the development of the entire world."[1] Fuller participation in international life, especially on the economic plane, was arguably one of the major developments in the Brezhnev era. Leonid Brezhnev, it has been said, "brought foreign policy home to the USSR," tying it more closely to domestic concerns and exposing the country to international and transnational currents as never before.[2]

If reciprocal domestic-foreign effects are certain to figure in Soviet politics in the decade ahead, the perplexing question is on what scale and with what significance. How, in concrete terms, will external events impinge on Soviet internal politics, and with what force will they make themselves felt on the prospects for moderate reform? In turn, what practical differences will the internal Soviet situation spell for Soviet foreign activity? And what, finally, are the implications for Western policy?

General Effects: Political Succession, Regime Goals, Constraints

We can begin by noting the three main ways Soviet domestic and foreign policy interact: by the recruitment of leaders, in the goals and aspirations of the regime, and through the constraining power of internal and external events on regime choices.

Political succession and foreign relations. A cardinal feature of Soviet politics today is the advent of new top leaders and of a younger elite generation. Political succession could both be affected by external events and exert a perceptible influence on Soviet foreign conduct.

The accession of Andropov and then Chernenko took place in an international climate marked by embittered East-West relations and by concurrent Soviet setbacks within the USSR's own camp (especially in Poland) and in selected parts of the Third World (notably in Afghanistan). Most dramatic was the clash with the United States. In both previous Soviet successions, a new American leader (Dwight Eisenhower in 1953, Lyndon Johnson in 1964) had recently pointed American policy in what Moscow saw as a markedly more combative direction. This time the situation was worse: the new occupant of the White House, Ronald Reagan, was out of deep conviction the most anti-Soviet chief executive since the 1940s, and the edge of American hostility was further honed by the widespread disillusionment over the unravelling of the U.S.-Soviet détente of the 1970s. Brezhnev was not far wide of the mark in observing at one of his final public appearances that the Soviet Union's global adversary had "deployed a political, ideological, and economic offensive" against it.[3]

The charged international atmosphere has had little apparent effect thus far on politics within the inner Soviet leadership. Andropov, it is true, had better foreign policy credentials than any of the other contenders in 1982, or indeed than any incoming General Secretary previously, and this may have served him well in the struggle for power. It is also conceivable, though unprovable, that a desire to present a united front against the Reagan crusade contributed to Andropov's tardiness in disposing of competing or superannuated Politburo colleagues such as Konstantin Chernenko and Nikolai Tikhonov. And yet, it was Chernenko, a man with negligible involvement with foreign policy, who took Andropov's place in 1984. As best we can ascertain, domestic considerations were decisive in the 1982 and 1984 rounds of the succession contest and are apt to be so again. Symptomatic of this is that the two favorites to follow Chernenko as head of the party, Mikhail Gorbachev and Grigori Romanov, have had even less exposure to international affairs than he has.

What has been and will be the reverse effect of leadership succession on Soviet foreign policy? As a general point, the same factors that propel the regime toward moderate internal reform also prod it to consider initiatives to break foreign policy log-jams. Politburo successions shake up coalitions and bring new individuals and teams into high office. They grease the machinery of policy change and often lead to a reaction against the less successful ideas of the previous leader. We see already some limited evidence of reappraisal of foreign policy under Andropov and Chernenko, particularly in the sweetening of Soviet proposals on arms control, in the hastened effort to mend fences with Peking, and in the several attempts to lessen frictions with the West (such as the five-year U.S.-Soviet grain deal, the signing of the Madrid accord on European security, the gestures on human rights, and recently Chernenko's call for a resumption of détente).

On the other hand, one can only be struck by how much more listless the regime's initiatives have been in foreign than in domestic policy. Many central elements of Brezhnev's policy have gone unaltered—witness the continuing quest for victory in Afghanistan (where the Soviets have now fought longer than in World War II), the paucity of progress in negotiations with China, the unyielding line in Poland, and the deterioration of relations with Washington in the fall of 1983, brought to a new nadir by the Korean Air Lines incident and the Soviet suspension of talks over limiting intermediate and strategic nuclear forces. Changes in key personnel have been avoided, and Moscow's chief international spokesman for the last quarter-century— the seventy-five-year-old Foreign Minister, Andrei Gromyko—has been upgraded in status (he became one of three first deputy chairmen of the Council of Ministers in March 1983).

Interpretations vary as to this relative immobility. One is that the new leaders want to make large changes in foreign policy but are unable to do so because of political opposition from within the Soviet establishment. This theory is not convincing, because Andropov and Chernenko both made brisk headway in consolidating their power, and their political standing has been sufficient for them to make a solid start on domestic innovations. We know that in the mid-1950s a new Soviet leader whose authority was no greater than that of the two new General Secretaries of the 1980s, Nikita Khrushchev, pushed through important foreign policy reforms (the Korean armistice, the Austrian peace treaty, the rapprochement with Tito's Yugoslavia, and overtures to the Third World) and, what is more, used these to help augment his prestige and win adherents within the party.

A more persuasive explanation is that the Soviet elite, and Andropov and Chernenko with it, has been less dissatisfied with recent foreign policy than with domestic policy. Particularly in the Third World, the second half of the 1970s was a time of external Soviet gains, with the acquisition of new clients in Indochina, Angola, Mozambique, Ethiopia, South Yemen, and Afghanistan. Present difficulties notwithstanding, external developments do not represent nearly the threat to the regime's vital interests that the internal economic slowdown and erosion of public morale do. Furthermore, the regime's objective opportunities for reversing setbacks are less in foreign than in domestic affairs. This is an unavoidable result of the difference between international and domestic politics: in the world of states, there is no common law or culture, and each player must live by his wits to an extent unheard of within civil society. The Soviet bosses respond to this contrast more than most leaders, for they are used to an abnormal degree of control in their domestic affairs. Vexing though Soviet society at times may be to them, it does not present them with challenges as maddeningly beyond their reach as those raised by a Ronald Reagan or an Anwar el-Sadat. Because the international environment is so complex and unpredictable, Soviet conservatives have an easier time arguing for constancy in foreign policy. The reformist impulse is weaker here than in domestic policy, the grip of inertia greater, and the difference between reformers and conservatives slighter.

Control over the supreme political positions aside, what of the more pervasive changeover of generations within the policy-making elite? In tandem with the bureaucracies concerned with internal affairs, the foreign policy establishment will, over the next five or ten years, come at all levels under the control of members of the post-Stalin generation. As in domestically oriented institutions, the newcomers are better educated and informed than their elders. They also have traveled far more widely abroad, including in the West, and tend to have fewer preconceptions about the evils of capitalism and the perfection of the Soviet system. In their published writings, at least, experts from the younger age groups subscribe to "a less theological, increasingly pragmatic and objective world outlook . . . endorse a more hopeful view of capitalist foreign policy than did their Stalinist predecessors . . . [are] more optimistic about the prospects for coexistence and accommodation . . . [and] seem to have developed a particularly acute appreciation of the advantages which a relaxed international atmosphere holds for Soviet diplomacy."[4] Within the limits posed by their acceptance of the fundamentals of Soviet ideology and superpower ambitions, these younger figures are inclined to be more interested than the old guard in good relations with the United States, in greater East-West contact, and (least clearly) in steps to manage the U.S. — Soviet tug-of-war in the non-aligned world.

Leadership and generational change thus hold out some prospect of the Soviets modifying certain of the more confrontational and less effective facets of their foreign behavior. The door to an adjustment in policy and style is more open under the post-Brezhnev Politburo than it has been in some time, although Andropov's cautious opening moves and the appallingly unsophisticated Soviet reaction to the political afterclap of the KAL affair warn us against assuming too much too soon. The influx of younger officials in the late 1980s should, other variables held constant, help moderate Soviet policy, albeit in ways at which we can only guess today. Because the amount of policy distress, however, is at present less in foreign than in domestic affairs, and the possibilities of real change more dependent on forces immune to Kremlin control, the changes stemming from political succession will in all likelihood be less pronounced than in internal policy.

The regime's goals, foreign and domestic.   Foreign and domestic agendas can also be linked by the objectives and aspirations of a country's political leadership. For example, politicians may decide that their domestic program has to be set aside because foreign problems are more pressing, or they may seek out adventures in foreign policy to distract public attention from their domestic troubles, or their ideologies or outlooks may prescribe reinforcing programs at home and abroad. Does any of these three examples apply to the Soviet regime over the next decade?

The first example is certainly not relevant. Andropov and Chernenko have taken more vigorous action on the domestic than on the foreign front, not less, indicating a bias toward internal issues that their successors will likely share. The political success of the top leaders will be determined in some measure by performance in foreign policy — but not at the expense of domestic issues. Andropov, for one, said that domestic improvement, vital in its own right, is also a prerequisite for success in foreign policy. "It is not difficult to understand," he told Moscow factory workers in early 1983, "that the greater our successes . . . [and] the better things stand in our national economy, then the sounder will be our international position."[5]

Nor should one suppose that the regime will look for diversions on foreign soil flashy enough to obscure domestic misery. In the past, hazardous ventures abroad have not been timed to ease the mood of the Soviet population. When they have been undertaken, say, the sending of Soviet pilots and air defense crews to Egypt in 1969–70 or the occupation of Afghanistan in 1979, they have been hushed up rather than played up in the Soviet media.

Can we foresee the third type of linkage, a broad sort of congruence between foreign and domestic goals? At a certain level of abstraction, some such harmony assuredly must be preserved. "It is virtually impossible," one eminent American authority on Soviet foreign policy writes, "to conceive of the Soviet system's survival in its present form were its rulers to abandon explicitly, or even implicitly, the main premises behind their foreign policy."[6] Many integral features of the USSR's domestic authoritarianism derive support from the Soviet doctrine of a divided world, in which American-led "imperialism" pursues nefarious designs against the USSR and its allies. Still, as the same scholar attests, the Soviets enjoy great tactical flexibility in defining the external situation of the moment. They fluctuate between two general perspectives on the world: one, analogous to that of the rentier in business, counsels caution, timely concessions to the United States, and a biding of time as investments pay off and contradictions within the opposing coalition ripen; the other, the mentality of the speculator, is in more of a hurry, more assertive and open to risk, and less skittish about resistance by the capitalist powers.[7]

Each of these orientations is consistent with the maintenance of core Soviet institutions, as each justifies a high degree of domestic control by the party and its agents. Historically, periods of militancy in foreign policy have not been clearly associated with internal repression and conservatism, nor has a more accommodating foreign policy necessarily coincided with domestic reformism.[8] In the decade to come, it is likely true that several of the more drastic (and more improbable) internal outcomes—such as revolutionary collapse or radical reform—would be incompatible with continuation of Soviet foreign policy in either its rentier or its speculator form. But moderate reform, the most plausible domestic path, is caught in no such bind, since it is trained on economic issues and not on the beliefs and myths underlying party rule. It would dovetail with either version of the basic Soviet foreign policy philosophy.

The rentier outlook, however, would make moderate reform somewhat easier, if for no other reason than it involves fewer gambles and obligations and leaves Soviet leaders a freer hand to attend to domestic problems. All things being equal, therefore, moderate reform should predispose the regime toward the less strident of the two broad foreign policy alternatives open to it. While scarcely embracing the international status quo or ceasing their opportunistic exploitation of what they call the shifting "correlation of forces," Soviet leaders are likely to be more concerned with getting their own house in order. Among other things, they will be more open to détente with the West and the United States—on the assumption, in Andropov's phrase, of "the necessity and mutual advantageousness of a lengthy peaceful coexistence of states with diverse social systems"—and more willing than they were in the 1970s to tone down Soviet expansionism in order to make détente possible.[9] This will be rationalized as the best means in the current setting of promoting ideologically sound goals. To quote Andropov in November 1982: "The steady uplift of our economy and the improvement of public welfare are both our duty before the Soviet people and our international duty." The party, Andropov said, using the words of a speech given by Lenin at the end of the Russian Civil War in 1921, has to be "guided by the Leninist dictum that we have our main influence on the world revolutionary process through our [domestic] economic policy."[10] In other words, turning a blind eye to domestic ills today may sacrifice Soviet power tomorrow and lessen the ultimate Soviet contribution to progressive change in the world.

Domestic and foreign problems as constraints on Soviet policy.   The Soviet preoccupation with problems at home and the arduous task of implementing even moderate reform should discourage a forward, high-cost stance in dealings with the West. The most noticeable change is likely to be fewer new commitments, particularly in the Third World. The Soviets are apt to be rather less primed than in the 1970s to seize opportunities and, because the anti-colonial revolution in Asia and Africa has now nearly spent itself, occasions for inexpensive extension of Soviet influence should be fewer in the decade ahead in any case. A Politburo occupied with political succession, fighting corruption, restructuring industry, and the like will have less time and energy for distant adventures. It will also be easier for the Soviet leadership to argue as Andropov did in June 1983 that "the social progress of these [developing] countries can . . . only be the result of the labor of their peoples and the correct policy of their leaderships."[11]

The Soviet attitude on standing commitments such as Afghanistan, the alliance with Syria, and the stormy negotiations over intermediate-range nuclear forces in Europe, however, promises to change less. There are good psychological reasons for this. The same feeling of vulnerability that prompts the Soviets to weigh internal reform and balk at added foreign responsibilities also puts them on guard against concessions on foreign policy giving the appearance (to either external or internal audiences) of lack of strength or will. A prickliness on this point is evident in Soviet statements today, which remonstrate noisily about "the plans of those who count on 'the weaknesses' of the Soviet Union."[12] It follows that Soviet cave-ins to pressure will be few and that there will be no Soviet pullbacks (in Afghanistan or anywhere else) unless face-saving formulas are found. Under no conditions will the Kremlin feel it need accept humiliation or abandon bedrock objectives.

Do foreign developments in turn constrain the Soviet leaders' ability to pursue their domestic goals? No one—certainly no one in Moscow with whom I have ever discussed the issue—doubts that an easing of international relations, and especially a thaw in relations with the United States, would lighten the political task of moderate Soviet reformers. Antagonism with foreign adversaries reinforces the Stalinist garrison mentality so closely connected with economic overcentralization and vigilance against criticism. In an environment of foreign policy crisis, certain moderate improvements would probably be ruled out entirely (such as cutting the defense budget), some changes would be delayed, others would be watered down for lack of adequate political and material resources, and generally the authoritarian aspects of the changes would be accentuated.

Extreme challenges from without might conceivably drive the regime completely away from moderate reform. One such challenge would be an assault on the established order in Eastern Europe. To achieve the maximum impact, this would have to involve—as it never has in the past—national uprisings culminating in Soviet military intervention in more than one country in the region. Mayhem in the East European empire might play into the hands of Soviet hardliners and superpatriots or, to the same effect, activate the survival instincts of middle-of-the-roaders in the regime. The leadership could then wind up declaring a bloc-wide state of siege, delegating new control powers to the army and KGB, and clamping down for a time on even whispers of reform.

Similar consequences could flow from an emergency in relations with the United States, and particularly one in which the Politburo came to the conclusion that the Americans were preparing to unleash a general war. A Moscow-Washington confrontation would most likely be sparked by a local conflict involving allies or proxies in a tinderbox region like the Persian Gulf, the Caribbean, or the Korean peninsula. No such scenario can be precluded for the 1980s and 1990s. But it would seem that the most likely forms of superpower sparring will not divert the regime from trying the kinds of limited internal improvements explored in Chapter 4 of this essay. Events since Brezhnev's death are instructive. Yuri Andropov obviously saw no inconsistency between acknowledging (and contributing to) an extraordinary level of East-West enmity—an ideological fray that he described as "unprecedented in the entire postwar period for its intensity and sharpness"—and getting a program of moderate domestic reform off the ground.[13] There probably are those in the Soviet hierarchy who see rawer conflict with the West (short of war) as constituting one of the strongest arguments for internal reform, on the premise that only a more efficient Soviet system can prevail in the long-term struggle with the capitalists.

Specific Effects: Five Hybrid Issues

Beyond the general interaction of foreign and domestic priorities, Soviet decision makers must deal with similar linkages in specific instances. Five of these will be touched on here: ethnic and regional problems; defense spending; foreign economic ties; change in Eastern Europe; and human rights. In each case we want to know how the internal and external aspects of the issue interlock and how they bear on moderate domestic reform.

Ethnic and regional questions. One cluster of internal problems of some significance to foreign policy has to do with relations among the Soviet Union's numerous ethnic groups and geographic units. It is probably true, for example, that the party's ambitious Siberian development projects of the 1960s and 1970s, among them the start in 1974 on construction of a second trans-Siberian railway, were designed in part to fortify Siberia against possible Chinese encroachment and to pave the way for Soviet-Japanese cooperation in extracting the region's mineral and energy riches. Thus, foreign policy considerations apparently favored the budgetary claims of Siberia, populated mainly by Russians, over those of such non-Russian areas as the Ukraine and Central Asia. Similarly, many have thought, the 1979 decision to invade Afghanistan was inspired partly by the Politburo's anxiety over the Islamic revival in Iran and Afghanistan spreading to Soviet republics like Uzbekistan and Tadzhikistan, and the condemnation of the rise of Solidarity by a fear of Polish events contaminating the Baltic republics.

In actuality, the interaction between foreign and domestic concerns of this sort has not been particularly strong in the recent Soviet past. It is not likely to be so in the immediate future, whether or not the Kremlin embarks on moderate internal reform. Concerning regional development, calculations of the domestic economic payoff rather than national security considerations have always been foremost in such Soviet decisions, including decisions about Siberia. While certain areas would profit greatly from massive foreign investment in Soviet resource development schemes—of the sort with which the Japanese declined involvement in the 1970s but which they continue to explore—precedent indicates that the Soviet authorities will approach such plans with an eye to maximizing the total benefits to the USSR, not to any individual region.[14]

The ethnic question also is but weakly connected to Soviet foreign policy appraisals. Soviet hostility to Solidarity was amply fueled by Solidarity itself and owed little to ethnic developments on the Soviet side of the border (which, in any event, have a vigorous life of their own in the Baltic region). The Moslem nationalities of Central Asia, which are of the greatest long-run worry to the Russian rulers, have to date found little if anything to admire in Khomeini-style fundamentalism. Soviet troops entered Afghanistan mostly to prevent a newly established satellite regime from leaving the Soviet orbit, and apprehensions about nearby Moslem areas in the Soviet Union appear to have had scant weight in the decision.[15] All things considered, external threats to the ethnic balance will be minimal in the decade to come, so long as Moscow's control over the non-Russian communities remains as sturdy as it has been. Moderate, economic-centered reform should not have much direct effect on either the Soviet ethnic problem or its relevance for foreign policy.

Defense spending.   It is clear that defense policy, at once a claimant on national treasure and a means of projecting Soviet power abroad, straddles the demarcation line between domestic and foreign issues. A modern military establishment never comes cheap, but for the USSR, with its traditional nervousness about invasion, its global ambitions, and its resolve to compete militarily with an American colossus which has almost double the Soviet economic capacity, the costs have been unique. Soviet military outlays stood at 13 or 14 percent of total GNP in the early 1980s. As a proportion of the national economy, they have for five decades exceeded the military spending of all other industrial countries (including the United States, where the ratio to GNP is some 7 percent).

At first glance, the faltering economy and the pressure of maintaining or improving rates of investment and mass consumption would seem to give the Soviet leaders ample reason to reduce the mammoth military budget. Will this, however, be the case? Will the needs of internal retrenchment and reform necessarily prompt them to slacken their military effort and exercise restraint abroad? There are no simple answers to these questions, and no automatic connection between the internal and external dimensions of the defense-spending issue.

For one thing, the regime has almost always given primacy to national security objectives in deciding on military appropriations. It reduced the rate of growth of military spending to around 2 percent in 1977, from 4 or 5 percent in the preceding decade, but this was during a period of still relatively relaxed East-West relations, and it could well be reversed under new circumstances. The leaders have consistently been prepared, even at moments of great domestic strain, to make formidable sacrifices to keep Soviet military readiness at the level dictated by perceived foreign policy needs, however inflated these may look to foreign observers. It can be inferred, therefore, that deep cuts in Soviet defense spending are not in the cards unless the Politburo comes to believe that external conditions, and above all relations with the United States, warrant them.

For another thing, there is no iron link between reductions in the military budget and domestic reform. Redirecting defense rubles to other needs would be only one of several items in a package of moderate reforms, and reform can be launched with or without it. Failure to slash military outlays would make economic reform more difficult but not impossible, and by keeping resource use taut it arguably would simply make some other aspects of economic reform more imperative. Further, a steady-state or even a leaner military establishment, were that to be accomplished, would not necessarily involve a more conciliatory Soviet foreign policy. In the Third World, at least, the Kremlin (like the White House) may find ways to use stable or smaller forces more efficiently and aggressively. The Soviet action that has most incensed the West—the occupation of Afghanistan— occurred at a time of reduced growth in Soviet military spending, and probably could be sustained by a Soviet military machine half its present size. From the point of view of American interests, it is worth noting that one element of defense spending that is among the least onerous in budgetary terms is the development and procurement of strategic nuclear weapons.[16] If the Soviets are to be more forthcoming in negotiations over these weapons—and there is good reason to think that they will be—it will be because they see arms control as a prudent security policy, not because they do not have the wherewithal to stay in the competition. If financial savings were the sole desideratum, the Soviet Union could recoup as much or more by achieving détente with China and demobilizing some of the mainly conventional forces (more than fifty divisions) stationed along the Chinese frontier since the late 1960s.

The Soviet leaders have long referred to defense spending as a burden on their economy, and lately they have repeated the claim that arms reductions would enable "the release of material resources senselessly wasted in the arms race" to other uses.[17] The regime's obsessive secrecy about national security matters makes it difficult to know how large they think the savings might be, but others have made rough estimates.

Most of these studies suggest that the economic benefits of cutbacks in Soviet defense spending would be surprisingly modest and slow to materialize. Consumption standards would be helped more than aggregate growth, but in neither case would the impact be great. A U.S. government report on the effects of zero growth in Soviet military spending over the remainder of the 1980s estimates that long lead times in converting military assembly lines, supply and transport bottlenecks, and other problems would limit the improvement in the annual rate of growth of GNP to somewhere between one-tenth and one-fifth of a percentage point through 1990. Per capita consumption would do a little better, rising by an extra 0.5 percent a year. Another analysis, by two private economists, looks at the effects of varying the annual increase in defense outlays up or down from the rate of 4 to 5 percent recorded from the mid-1960s through 1976. With defense spending at the pre-1977 baseline, Soviet GNP would increase in the latter half of the 1980s by 2.2 percent a year and consumption per capita by 0.1 percent a year. Defense growth of only 2.5 percent a year, roughly its post-1976 rate, leaves GNP growth unchanged and boosts consumption growth to a still puny 0.6 percent a year. The most interesting outcome is of an acceleration of Soviet defense expenditures. If they grew by 7.5 percent a year, there would still be little impact on GNP (up 2.1 percent a year), but per capita consumption would *go down* by 1.0 percent a year. Under this projection, the defense sector would by 1990 comprise 22 percent of the entire economy, defense production would account for 65 percent of all new output, and the total stock of new machinery produced by Soviet workers would be delivered to the armed forces.[18]

Two conclusions emerge from these figures, each consistent with my earlier prediction that domestic factors will not soon compel the Soviets to rethink standing policy commitments but may discourage new adventures. First, the economic implications of failing to cut the defense budget are not catastrophic. The burden of either the most recent tempo of increase or the somewhat higher rate sustained before 1977, while heavy for state and society, is probably bearable, and lowering it would be no panacea for Soviet economic problems. Yet, second, the consequences of upping the rate of growth of military expenditures are much more chilling from the Kremlin's perspective. If the regime insists on quickening its military buildup in the 1980s, the result will in all probability be an absolute decline in living standards, a very different situation from slow growth or even stagnation. This is not a prospect that even the most hawkish Politburo could contemplate with equanimity. The Soviet leadership, while perhaps being prepared to persevere in the arms race, is almost certain to be receptive to reasonable accommodation with the West, saving it from running faster than it can safely run.

Foreign economic ties.   A steady move away from economic autarchy is one distinctive legacy of the Soviet 1960s and 1970s. The ratio of imports to GNP, which was less than 1 percent in the isolationist 1930s and about 3 percent in the mid-1960s, climbed to roughly 5 percent at the beginning of the 1980s, low by world standards but high by Russian standards. Especially large was the growth posted in trade with the industrialized Western countries. Western imports rose from 20 percent of the Soviet total in 1965 to approximately 35 percent in the early 1980s. Procurements were massive of Western grain and of machinery and equipment for the automotive, fertilizer, petroleum, and other industries embodying a higher level of technology than that prevalent in the USSR.[19] Although precise calculation of the effect of increased trade on the Soviet economy is difficult, there is general agreement that it has been of substantial benefit. It has been said, to take one estimate, that the $7 billion the Soviets spent on grain imports in 1982 was $32 billion less than it would have cost them to produce the extra grain themselves. According to a British economist, imports of advanced Western equipment netted the Soviet economy about one-half a percent a year in additional growth in the 1970s, and some Western experts put it higher than that.[20]

One could well imagine a strategy for internal Soviet reform that placed a high value on expanding foreign economic ties and coupled this to modernization of domestic industry. Importing more high-technology goods would be the centerpiece of such a strategy, supplemented perhaps by greater contacts with foreign scientists and industrialists, joint ventures with foreign capital, grooming certain industries for export production at world prices, and maybe even applying for admission to the International Monetary Fund. Such a program, attractive though it may look on paper, seems improbable.

One negative factor is the deterioration of the conditions that assisted the rapid expansion of Soviet imports in the 1960s and 1970s. This trend was taking hold well before Brezhnev's death. Growth in trade with the Western nations, which was 28 percent a year from 1971 to 1975, slowed to 16 percent a year from 1976 to 1980 and 9 percent a year in 1981–82, and the official plan (which now looks unrealistic) has it averaging a mere 2 percent in 1981–85.[21] Worsening relations with the West, and the United States in particular, help account for the drop—a situation apt to improve only slowly, if at all, in the near future—but the most important explanation is the poor performance of Soviet hard currency earnings, the USSR's preferred way of financing imports. These jumped with world oil and gold prices after 1973 (mineral fuels are by far the biggest Soviet export to the West), only to level off at the end of the 1970s when these prices sagged. The prognosis is that the Soviets will do well over the next decade to hold hard-currency earnings at their present level, using exports of natural gas to Western Europe to offset a predicted drop in oil exports.[22]

In theory, the Soviets could achieve a big increase in foreign trade the way many of their East European allies did in the 1970s: by borrowing more heavily from foreign governments and banks. In practice, this path is all but closed. In the post-détente age, most Western governments have little interest in underwriting major new Soviet borrowing, and private lenders are being deterred by the general crisis in international finance and by Poland's wretched performance with its huge debt. The Soviet leaders, who are congenitally cautious about foreign borrowing, seem determined not to see their current obligations to the West — $10.1 billion as of January 1983, as compared to under $600 million in 1971 — swell much further. This resolve already seems firmer now than it was under Brezhnev, if one is to judge from Soviet commentary on NATO's plans to use a "credit trap" to increase Soviet indebtedness and susceptibility to Western pressure.[23]

The debt question aside, the regime has given signs since the late 1970s of growing disenchantment with East-West commerce, and in particular with imports of high-technology machinery. Nothing seems likely to reverse that mood in the period ahead. Even pro-reform advisers long favorable to greater trade now concede that the Soviet Union is today "forced to approach collaboration with the West more selectively."[24] Both conservatives and reformists have been affected by two considerations: first, a backlash against the failure of the United States to deliver on the most-favored-nation status for tariffs and sharply expanded trade promised in the early 1970s, and against the several partial trade embargoes led later by Presidents Carter and Reagan; and second, a more deep-seated recalculation of the economic dividends of technology transfer. Western imports, it is now being stated widely in the Soviet media, are ultimately not a substitute for indigenous Soviet technology, and are often utilized ineffectively themselves because of poor Soviet planning and management. Therefore, the argument goes, the Soviet Union will get better results by improving its own science and industry, and its capacity to assimilate better current levels of imports, than by trying to bypass the problem by bigger purchases abroad.

The prospect of static or perhaps reduced trade with the West does not obstruct the chances of moderate Soviet reform. Soviet-Western trade thrived under a Brezhnev regime that refused to make more than minimal changes at home and seemed often to see imports as a way of avoiding more systematic improvements. Brezhnev's heirs, with less access to the implicit short-term subsidies provided by expanded imports, now have all the more reason to direct their main energies to moderate domestic reform.

For the West, this turn of events can mean only one thing: less and not more opportunity to alter Soviet conduct by economic means. Western economic leverage over the Soviet Union was never great to begin with, on account of Western disunity and the Soviets' low dependence on foreign trade. In 1980 total Soviet imports came to 5.0 percent of the country's GNP, imports from the West to 1.7 percent, and imports from the United States to an insignificant 0.1 percent. If, as can be anticipated, the already low importance of imports to Soviet strategy declines, so will the capacity of Western governments to exercise short-term economic influence over Soviet policy.

Eastern Europe. Because the six allied states in Eastern Europe are politically, economically, and militarily so closely tied to their Soviet patron, their internal affairs and foreign policies are separated by only a porous boundary from the domestic concerns of the Soviet leadership.

Circumstances in Eastern Europe differ in several ways from those during previous periods of political succession in the Soviet Union. First, the viability of the communist regime of the most important country in the area, Poland, is in doubt after almost four years of turmoil. Some kind of pro-Soviet government will remain in power in Warsaw, but rule by an orthodox communist party, such as existed before the hammer blows of the Solidarity rebellion and military takeover, may not be seen again for years to come, if ever. Second, all of the USSR's partners from the Baltic to the Black Sea are mired in severe economic difficulties, ranging from acute crisis in Poland (which may not regain 1978 production levels until 1990) to a growth deceleration of Soviet dimensions in some of the other countries. Total hard-currency indebtedness was $58.3 billion in 1981 (it had been only $6.0 billion in 1970).[25] Third, the East European economies are receiving subsidies from Moscow far surpassing those in earlier Soviet successions, transfers that crimp the Soviet Union's ability to minister to its own economic ills. Soviet aid, mostly in the form of marketings of petroleum at prices below world par, peaked in 1981 at $21.1 billion and is scheduled to fall to $17.5 billion by 1985, still a sizable sum.[26] Fourth, economic difficulties are forcing at least debates over moderate economic reform in almost all the bloc countries. While few leaderships are likely to go as far as the Hungarians have, even regimes as conservative as the Czechoslovak and Rumanian are discussing serious changes.

How will the Soviets respond to this welter of problems? Two immediate policies inherited from Brezhnev will definitely be carried through. One is to bring continuing pressure to bear on the Polish regime and nation to refrain from repeating the Solidarity experiment. The enormity of Poland's foreign debt may give Western governments some small means of discouraging Soviet-backed repression, by manipulating negotiations over repayment and supplementary credits. The other urgent Soviet priority is to reduce the East European drag on the Soviet economy. Soviet planners have begun to do so, mainly by cutting oil deliveries, hiking energy prices, and requiring that customers unable to afford the increases enter into explicit credit arrangements to cover the shortfall.

But what of the longer haul? Is a more comprehensive strategy taking shape, and would it be affected by execution of a program of moderate reform within the Soviet Union? There are some signs that, despite Soviet opposition to Solidarity, Moscow has not foreclosed economic and social changes in Eastern Europe. Andropov stressed that "big differences in economics, in culture, and in the ways and methods of developing socialism" are inescapable within the bloc. "This is natural, even if at times it seemed to us that [the development of communism] would be more uniform."[27] Other Soviet spokesmen, one presumes with Politburo clearance, have described East European reforms as essential, spoken approvingly of how "these reforms are taking on a more radical (*radikalnyi*) character," and emphasized that "each country [in the alliance] has its particularities" and that reforms can be expected to "differ in terms of depth, tempo of implementation, complexity, and many concrete features."[28]

If Soviet tolerance of policy innovation in Eastern Europe is increasing, Moscow also has a list of specific Soviet interests to promote. It wants to reduce energy subsidies further after 1985 and is openly twisting its allies' arms to produce more food for Soviet cupboards and to accept greater coordination of industrial and science strategies. It is demanding an end to increases in hard-currency indebtedness. It also is more anxious than ever about monitoring and controlling domestic change in the bloc countries, especially in the political dimension. The limits to acceptable change may be wider in the years to come, but the Soviets also intend them to be more meticulously observed. Soviet conservatives fear, of course, that another Prague Spring or Solidarity may be the surprise result of national experimentation. But it is also pro-reform officials and specialists in Moscow who advocate greater "exchange of experience," mutual consultation, and Soviet supervision of local developments.[29] Evidently they count on East European reform to demonstrate the practicality of analogous changes to Soviet skeptics, and they dread that botched reforms or loss of political control by any of the client parties will make the work of moderate reformers within the Soviet Union harder. The emerging Soviet design for Eastern Europe is thus not unlike the blueprint for moderate change at home: greater economic diversity and dynamism, but as much if not more political conformity among the populace. It remains to be seen whether Soviet leaders can make such a two-track strategy work.

Human rights. No Soviet domestic issue was more internationalized in the Brezhnev years than that of human rights. Two sides of this multifaceted question acquired particular prominence: government treatment of political dissidents, individuals openly discontented with the Soviet system; and emigration of Soviet citizens, something which had been practically impossible for most of Soviet history but in the 1970s was permitted for about 400,000 persons, about two-thirds of them Jews. The human rights issue mattered most in relations with the United States, where initially Congress and private groups took the lead but eventually Presidents Carter and Reagan, too, espoused the cause. American elite and mass attitudes toward the Soviet Union were greatly affected by Soviet behavior, as were the course of U.S.–Soviet economic relations and the timing if not the substance of American arms control proposals. The Soviets, for their part, reluctantly accepted the need to bargain over aspects of human rights as a price of dealing with Washington, and used carefully rationed concessions to secure American favor and repressive measures to convey displeasure with American policy.

The limited East-West dialogue over human rights all but ended after the Soviet invasion of Afghanistan, as Jewish emigration fell sharply, prominent dissidents were jailed and exiled, and new restrictions were slapped on postal, telephone, and radio communication. Under Yuri Andropov, who as KGB chief was responsible for implementation of the post-Afghanistan crackdown, the hard line was continued and even stiffened. There is little chance of it softening soon. Domestic reforms of some genre may be on the horizon, but these are being proposed only in economic and socioeconomic areas and will not involve liberalization, to say nothing of democratization, in the political and cultural fields. Moreover, as suggested in Chapter 4, the regime may well decide that an era of moderate internal reform, with all its attendant divisions and stresses, will require that certain individual freedoms be further curtailed, not enlarged. Wholesale violence of the sort under Stalin is unlikely and maybe even impossible, but the regime doubtless will be quick to stamp out any popular resistance to new economic and socioeconomic policies. At such a time, the authorities may also want to limit cultural contact with the West as much as possible.

This does not mean that foreign governments can have no influence on Soviet human rights policy. In spite of its generally rigid line at home, the post-Brezhnev regime has hinted at some flexibility. It withdrew the Soviet Union from the World Psychiatric Association in the spring of 1983, mostly, it seems, to prevent investigation of the use of mental clinics and prisons against political dissidents. Later in 1983, however, it also signalled publicly and privately that Jewish emigration might be resumed and prominent dissidents like Andrei Sakharov allowed to leave, and it granted visas to a family of Siberian Pentacostalists who had lived in the U.S. embassy in Moscow for years awaiting exit permission. It also made concessions at the Madrid review of the Helsinki agreements on European security, giving slightly fuller paper assurances on family reunification and foreign journalists' rights and agreeing to a new round of discussion at experts' meetings on human rights and human contacts to be convened in 1985 and 1986.

Western efforts to sway the Soviets on human rights abuses must continue, but they must also keep in mind three painful realities. First, partial and highly selective improvements are the most to be expected. The regime may be persuaded to bend its rules in particular instances—usually for people fortunate enough to have articulate defenders in the Western democracies—but external influence thus far has had almost no impact on the rules themselves. It is a delusion to imagine that Western leaders can negotiate a liberalization of the Soviet system even in the sunniest East-West climate. Second, Soviet willingness to accommodate Western pleas is likely to be considerably less in the near future than it has been in the past. And third, the best tactic for achieving such limited results as are attainable is one of quiet diplomacy and behind-the-scenes pressure. Attempts to dictate Soviet emigration policy, such as the 1974 Jackson-Vanik amendment to the U.S. Trade Reform Act, will be even less successful in future than they have been in the past.

Implications for Western Policy

Coping with the Soviet Union has always been difficult for Western societies, and it will not be less so in the coming decade. While sensitivity to the domestic agenda facing Soviet leaders may not tell us all we need to know in designing U.S. and allied policy, it does help inform policy in important respects. Several insights flow from a hard look at the Soviet system as it is and as it is likely to evolve.

First, we must be realistic about internal conditions in the Soviet Union. Western decision makers, especially in Washington, have vacillated in recent years between two contrary and equally misleading images of the Soviet Union. One treats it as a country of almost supernatural strength, a monolith ruled by obdurate ideologists who pay no heed to public wants and are at liberty to proceed with foreign adventures and conquests as they please. In the other image, the USSR is, as President Reagan said of it in his June 1982 address to the British Parliament, "inherently unstable," a society riddled with conflicts and tensions and experiencing a "great revolutionary crisis," which before long will climax in the downfall of its institutions.[30]

Neither impression bears much resemblance to Soviet reality and neither forms a reliable foundation for Western policy. The Soviet system today is stable in its fundamentals. The USSR is not Poland—its regime is far older, stronger, wilier, and more generally accepted by the average citizen. There is no revolutionary crisis in the Soviet Union today. Nor is there total mastery over events by the regime or an ability on its part to disregard utterly the demands of the population. The ruling party gives every indication of turning onto a road of moderate internal reform in which economic and socioeconomic policies will be seriously retooled in an effort to revive economic growth and improve popular welfare. The authoritarian Soviet system is responding to problems that have been brewing for some time, reflecting a capacity for change and for averting a collapse in which everything will change.

Second, internal factors make moderation in Soviet foreign behavior more likely but not necessary. In a time of political succession, economic woes, and limited domestic reform, the Soviet leaders will be re-evaluating unsuccessful and self-defeating policies as well as avoiding additional undertakings abroad. Western statesmen are thus in a better position today to work toward containing and accommodating Soviet power than they were in recent times. It is crucial to realize, however, that there is no absolute necessity for the Soviets to modify their foreign policy for domestic reasons, and no grounds for thinking that they will make important concessions on established points of controversy because of them.

Partial domestic reform can be pursued with or without shifts in foreign policy. The USSR is not strong enough to keep on piling up costly foreign commitments or to step up the arms race, but it is strong enough to persevere with most of its existing commitments. Awareness of Soviet liabilities must not blind us to Soviet assets. The USSR is still the largest country on the globe and ranks first in the size of its army, second in economic strength, and third in population. The Soviet bear may have an ache in its belly and a limp in its gait. This still leaves it a very big bear, with teeth and claws and a tough hide to match. It is far from being crippled, and, if cornered, it will be dangerous.

Third, we have a limited capacity to influence the Soviet domestic system. If moderate reform does indeed occur in the Soviet Union, this will be chiefly due to trends and pressures from within. In the short term, the West's leverage over Soviet domestic developments is not great. Loose talk about destabilizing the Soviet system is at best a diversion from the practical business of foreign policy, and at worst a flight from reason inviting a comparably immoderate response from Moscow. Economic boycotts, arms buildups, propaganda offensives, intervention on behalf of specific domestic groups, and the like may or may not deter or punish specific Soviet foreign policy decisions. But they have little potential for influencing in a way congenial to Western interests the domestic environment within which such decisions take place. If anything, they have less promise of doing so today than they did one or two decades ago.

American liberals sometimes propose that a set of more affirmative measures—expanded trade, scientific contacts, and so forth—be used to rehabilitate the Soviet system, lending support to its development in the direction of greater social and political pluralism. Unfortunately, carrots from the West can be used to equal effect by Soviet reformers or counter-reformers. We have little control over the result. Moreover, changes of any genuine significance gestate over long periods. Altered attitudes and values take generations; they cannot be reformed from year to year.

The ultimate Western resource for influencing Soviet society is not grain, optical fibers, or gas turbines but the slow-acting magnet of Western culture.[31] The essence of that culture is a belief in the sovereignty of the individual. Russian rulers since the reign of Peter the Great in the early eighteenth century have sought to trade with the West without buying, indeed, guarding against, this core value. Modern communications make the screen more penetrable, yet the pace of change will be glacial at best. It can be speeded up only a bit by external effort, and then only in a climate of improved political relations between East and West. Political détente, if it can be arranged, gives slightly, but only slightly, freer play to those irreverent forces—in literature, modern music, sport, the laboratory, and elsewhere—that celebrate the individual's right to think and act for himself.

Fourth, we should address Soviet foreign behavior directly, not indirectly by way of Soviet society. Efforts to affect the internal evolution of the Soviet Union are no proper replacement for a coherent program for curbing Soviet mischief abroad and encouraging a constructive Soviet approach to disputed issues and common interests. If the USSR were a bit player on the world stage, we might afford the luxury of trying to remake its institutions in the image of our own, but it is not. Whatever our admiration for those who oppose it from within, our interests give us no alternative to dealing sensibly with it as it exists. George Kennan, the dean of American Sovietologists, speaks the truth:

> American sympathies are, of course, engaged in behalf of people who fall afoul of any great political police system. This neither requires nor deserves any concealment. But, if what we are talking about is the official interrelationship of great governments, a choice must be made between the interests of democratization in Russia and the interests of world peace. In the face of this choice, there can be only one answer. Democracy is a matter of tradition, of custom, of what people are used to, of what they understand and respect. It is not something that can be suddenly grafted onto an unprepared people—particularly not from outside, and particularly not by precept, preaching, and pressure rather than by example. It is not a concept familiar to the mass of the Russian people; and whoever subordinates the interests of world peace

to the chimera of an early democratization of the Soviet Union will assuredly sacrifice the first of those values without promoting the second. By the nature of things, democratization not only can but must wait; world peace cannot.[32]

Little faith should be invested in the false notion that we can soon tame Soviet foreign behavior by changing Soviet society. The West's best means for addressing Soviet power are the same as they have always been: economic strength, cohesion around democractic principles, sufficient military power, and intelligent use of the traditional instruments of statecraft and balance of power. As usual, the leading role must be taken by the United States. So long as it seeks safety and not superiority, American policy has it well within its means to succeed. There is room for both superpowers, and their mutual security can be fashioned from a reasonable regard for each side's national security. Even with that accomplished, the rivalry between the two camps, rooted in different ideals and experiences, will continue, finding new forms of expression and levying new costs that the Soviets are not likely to shirk. The United States and the Western democracies need not fear their ability to compete, though everyone has reason to fear a competition that cannot be kept peaceful. Opposing Soviet aggression and balancing Soviet strength are necessary elements of Western strategy. They should be undertaken calmly and honestly, in a spirit that neither trivializes the Soviet challenge nor fantasizes it to be the source of all that ails the world. Equally vital are negotiations over mutually acceptable means of defusing the military component of the East-West contest, ground rules in the Third World, and ways of safeguarding common human values. Provided the United States and the allies retain their self-confidence and sense of proportion, a balanced policy toward a changing Soviet Union promises gratifying, if less than perfect, results.

Notes

Notes to Chapter 1. Brezhnev's Ambiguous Legacy

1. *Pravda,* November 13, 1982, p. 2. The speaker was Konstantin Chernenko.

2. L. I. Brezhnev, *Vospominaniya* (Memoirs) (Moscow: Politizdat, 1981), p. 16.

3. T. H. Rigby, "The Soviet Leadership: Towards a Self-Stabilizing Oligarchy?" *Soviet Studies,* 22 (October 1970), p. 175.

4. *XXV syezd Kommunisticheskoi partii Sovetskogo Soyuza: stenograficheskii otchot* (The 25th Congress of the Communist Party of the Soviet Union: Stenographic Record) (Moscow: Politizdat, 1976), I, 186–187.

5. *Pravda,* December 20, 1981, p. 1.

6. Quotation from Jerry F. Hough, *Soviet Leadership in Transition* (Washington, D.C.: Brookings Institution, 1980), p. 64. The calculation on Politburo turnover is my own (1.3 demotions a year under Khrushchev, 0.4 under Brezhnev).

7. L. I. Brezhnev, *Leninskim kursom: rechi i statyi* (On the Leninist Course: Speeches and Articles) (Moscow: Politizdat, 1970–83), III, 307.

8. Ibid., I, 22.

9. See Amy W. Knight, "The Powers of the Soviet KGB," *Survey,* 25 (Summer 1980), pp. 138–155.

10. *Pravda,* May 10, 1981, p. 2.

11. I. Bagramyan, "Rol' traditsii v vospitanii molodyozhi" (The Role of Tradition in the Upbringing of Youth), *Partiinaya zhizn,* no. 24 (December 1981), p. 52.

12. Roy A. Medvedev, *On Stalin and Stalinism* (Oxford: Oxford University Press, 1979), pp. 178–182.

13. This point is argued in Jack V. Haney, "The Revival of Interest in the Russian Past in the Soviet Union," *Slavic Review,* 32 (March 1973), pp. 1–16.

14. T. H. Rigby, "Forward From 'Who Gets What, When, How,'" ibid., 39 (June 1979), p. 206.

15. Zhores A. Medvedev, *The Rise and Fall of T. D. Lysenko* (New York: Columbia University Press, 1969), chaps. 9–10.

16. See for instance Peter H. Solomon, Jr., *Soviet Criminologists and Criminal Policy: Specialists in Policy-Making* (New York: Columbia University Press, 1978); Ronald J. Hill, *Soviet Politics, Political Science and Reform* (Oxford: Martin Robertson, 1980); Thane Gustafson, *Reform in Soviet Politics: Lessons of Recent Policies on Land and Water* (Cambridge: Cambridge University Press, 1981).

17. As one perceptive analyst wrote midway through the Brezhnev period, there had been "virtually no conceivable proposal for incremental change in party policy . . . that has not been aired in the Soviet press." Jerry F. Hough, "The Soviet System: Petrifaction or Pluralism?" *Problems of Communism,* 21 (March-April 1972), p. 31.

18. Paul Cocks, "Rethinking the Organizational Weapon: The Soviet System in a Systems Age," *World Politics,* 32 (January 1980), p. 251.

19. Jane P. Shapiro, "Soviet Consumer Policy in the 1970s: Plan and Performance," in Donald R. Kelley, ed., *Soviet Politics in the Brezhnev Era* (New York: Praeger, 1980), p. 106.

20. Gertrude E. Schroeder, "Soviet Living Standards: Achievements and Prospects," in Joint Economic Committee, U.S. Congress, *Soviet Economy in the 1980s: Problems and Prospects* (Washington, D.C.: GPO, 1983), II, 370.

21. Angel O. Bryne, James E. Cole, Thomas Brickerton, and Anton F. Malish, "U.S.-U.S.S.R. Grain Trade," ibid., p. 64.

22. There is some controversy over this. One commonly used index for the earnings distribution, the so-called decile ratio, shows greater inequality after 1968; comparison of the earnings of workers with white-collar personnel in industry, a better measure, shows greater equality. See Michael Ellman, "A Note on the Distribution of Earnings in the USSR Under Brezhnev," *Slavic Review,* 39 (December 1980), pp. 666–671; Alec Nove, "Income Distribution in the USSR: A Possible Explanation of Some Recent Data," *Soviet Studies,* 34 (April 1982), pp. 286–288; Jerry F. Hough, "Soviet Succession: Issues and Personalities," *Problems of Communism,* 31 (September-October 1982), pp. 25–26.

23. Richard J. Vidmer, "Soviet Studies of Organization and Management: A 'Jungle' of Competing Views," *Slavic Review,* 40 (Fall 1981), p. 409.

24. This was the phrase used by Zbigniew Brzezinski in his article "The Soviet Political System: Transformation or Degeneration?" *Problems of Communism,* 15 (January-February 1966), pp. 1–15.

25. Brezhnev, *Leninskim kursom,* VI, 245–246, 249.

26. A. G. Aganbegyan in *Literaturnaya gazeta,* May 4, 1977, p. 11.

27. Brezhnev, *Leninskim kursom,* VIII, 210.

28. Ibid., V, 527; VII, 254, 533; *XXVI syezd Kommunisticheskoi partii Sovetskogo Soyuza: stenograficheskii otchot* (The 26th Congress of the Communist Party of the Soviet Union: Stenographic Record) (Moscow: Politizdat, 1981), I, 67.

Notes to Chapter 2. What Ails the Soviet System?

1. *Pravda,* April 23, 1982, p. 2. As can be seen, Andropov made this particular statement before becoming head of the party.

2. Ibid., December 22, 1982, p. 2.

3. Murray Feshbach, "The Soviet Union: Population Trends and Dilemmas," *Population Bulletin,* 37 (August 1981), pp. 11, 13, 26, 30; quotation at p. 30. Background data on infant and adult mortality are in Christopher Davis and Murray Feshbach, "Rising Infant Mortality in the U.S.S.R. in the 1970s," *International Population Reports,* series P-95, no. 74 (Washington, D.C.: U.S. Bureau of the Census, Foreign Demographic Analysis Division, 1980); and John C. Dutton, Jr., "Causes of Soviet Adult Mortality Increases," *Soviet Studies,* 33 (October 1981), pp. 548–559.

4. Growth statistics from Central Intelligence Agency figures in Joint Economic Committee, U.S. Congress, *USSR: Measures of Economic Growth and Development, 1950–80* (Washington, D.C.: GPO, 1982), pp. 15, 259, 326; and Central Intelligence Agency, Office of Soviet Analysis, "USSR: Economic Trends and Policy Developments," briefing paper for Joint Economic Committee, U.S. Congress (Washington, D.C.: Processed, September 1983), pp. 29–33. CIA and other Western measures of Soviet economic performance do not coincide with Soviet measures, but the trends are the same throughout. Projections for consumption taken from Daniel Bond and Herbert Levine, eds., "The 11th Five-Year Plan, 1981–85," in Seweryn Bialer and Thane Gustafson, eds., *Russia at the Crossroads: The 26th Congress of the CPSU* (London: George Allen & Unwin, 1982), p. 100. I use the lower range of the Bond-Levine projections, based on low productivity growth, because without reform low productivity growth seems most likely for the 1980s.

5. Charles E. Lindblom, *Politics and Markets: The World's Political-Economic Systems* (New York: Basic Books, 1977), chap. 5.

6. Joint Economic Committee, *USSR,* pp. 20, 22; Gertrude E. Schroeder, *Consumption in the USSR: An International Comparison,* study prepared for Joint Economic Committee, U.S. Congress (Washington, D.C.: GPO, 1981), p. 18. Schroeder rated the Soviet standard of living at 34 percent of the American level in 1976, up only 6 percent from 1955.

7. Bond and Levine, p. 89; Central Intelligence Agency, "USSR," p. 2.

8. Anthony Downs, *Inside Bureaucracy* (Boston: Little, Brown, 1967), p. 160.

9. L. I. Brezhnev, *Leninskim kursom: rechi i statyi* (On the Leninist Course: Speeches and Articles) (Moscow: Politizdat, 1970–83), II, 99–100.

10. Timothy J. Colton, "Making Policy for Soviet Urban Development," paper delivered at annual meeting of the American Association for the Advancement of Slavic Studies, Monterey, California, September 1981.

11. Loren R. Graham, "Reasons for Studying Soviet Science: The Example of Genetic Engineering," in Linda L. Lubrano and Susan G. Solomon, eds., *The Social Context of Soviet Science* (Boulder, Colorado: Westview Press, 1980), pp. 235–236.

12. The reactive nature of the decision is stressed in Boris Rumer, "The 'Second' Agriculture in the USSR," *Soviet Studies,* 33 (October 1981), pp. 560–572.

13. *Pravda*, December 22, 1982, p. 2.

14. Paul A. Goble, "Ideology, Methodology, and Nationality: The USSR Academy of Sciences Council on Nationality Problems," paper delivered at annual meeting of the American Political Science Association, Washington, D.C., August 1980.

15. S. Enders Wimbush, "The Russian Nationalist Backlash," *Survey*, 24 (Summer 1979), p. 37.

16. V. Z. Rogovin, "Sotsialnaya politika i yeyo vliyaniye na obshchestvennyye nravy" (Social Policy and its Influence on Public Mores), *Voprosy filosofii*, no. 8 (August 1978), p. 12.

17. Feshbach, "The Soviet Union," p. 2; and same author, "Trends in the Soviet Muslim Population—Demographic Aspects," in Joint Economic Committee, U.S. Congress, *Soviet Economy in the 1980s: Problems and Prospects* (Washington, D.C.: GPO, 1983), II, 305.

18. Walter D. Connor, "Generations and Politics in the USSR," *Problems of Communism*, 24 (September-October 1975), p. 27.

19. The effect has been greatest on rural television viewers, for whom "the urban life they see portrayed on television throws into startling relief the tremendous disparities between town and country." Ellen Propper Mickiewicz, *Media and the Russian Public* (New York: Praeger Special Studies, 1980), p. 39.

20. Murray Yanowitch, "Schooling and Inequalities," in Leonard Schapiro and Joseph Godson, eds., *The Soviet Worker: Illusions and Realities* (London: Macmillan, 1981), p. 134; and more generally Gail Warshofsky Lapidus, "Social Trends," in Robert Byrnes, ed., *After Brezhnev: Sources of Soviet Conduct in the 1980s* (Bloomington: Indiana University Press, 1983), pp. 200–210.

21. *Literaturnaya gazeta*, January 8, 1975, p. 11.

22. Ibid.

23. *Trud*, May 30, 1981, p. 2.

24. T. I. Zaslavskaya, "Ekonomicheskoye povedeniye i ekonomicheskoye razvitiye" (Economic Behavior and Economic Development), *Ekonomika i organizatsiya promyshlennogo proizvodstva*, no. 3 (March 1980), pp. 19–20.

25. Maurice Friedberg, "Soviet Letters Under Brezhnev," *Problems of Communism*, 29 (May-June 1980), p. 53.

26. T. I. Zaslavskaya and L. L. Rybakovskii, "Protsessy migratsii i ikh regulirovaniye v sotsialisticheskom obshchestve" (Migration Processes and their Regulation in a Socialist Society), *Sotsiologicheskiye issledovaniya*, no. 1 (January–March 1978), p. 62.

27. Figures from Vladimir G. Treml, *Alcohol in the USSR: A Statistical Study* (Durham, N.C.: Duke Press Policy Studies, 1982).

28. Igor Birman, "The Financial Crisis in the USSR," *Soviet Studies*, 32 (January 1980), pp. 84–105.

29. "So much pressure has been created in demand for certain goods that the purchaser is starting to take for a reserve up to fifteen or twenty pairs of nylons or stockings, large amounts of cloth and thread, etc. In such a situation, the consumer himself worsens the shortage." *Literaturnaya gazeta*, September 26, 1979, p. 10.

30. Zaslavskaya, "Ekonomicheskoye povedeniye," pp. 28–29.

31. *Pravda,* June 16, 1983, p. 2. Valuable general accounts are Gregory Grossman, "The 'Second Economy' of the USSR," *Problems of Communism,* 26 (September-October 1977), pp. 25–40; Aron Katsenelinboigen, "Coloured Markets in the Soviet Union," *Soviet Studies,* 29 (January 1977), pp. 62–85; Dennis O'Hearn, "The Consumer Second Economy: Size and Effects," ibid., 32 (April 1980), pp. 218–234; Dimitri K. Simes, "The Soviet Parallel Market," *Survey,* 21 (Summer 1975), pp. 42–52.

32. S. Kheinman, "XXVI syezd KPSS i strategiya intensifikatsii" (The 26th Congress of the CPSU and the Strategy of Intensification), *Kommunist,* no. 3 (February 1982), p. 27.

33. *Pravda,* June 16, 1983, p. 2. There are dozens of revealing anecdotes about corruption in a new book by a former Soviet lawyer: Konstantin M. Simis, *USSR: The Corrupt Society* (New York: Simon and Schuster, 1982).

34. Gertrude E. Schroeder, "The Soviet Economy on a Treadmill of 'Reforms,'" in Joint Economic Committee, U.S. Congress, *Soviet Economy in a Time of Change* (Washington, D.C.: GPO, 1979), I, 313.

35. Seymour E. Goodman, "Soviet Computing and Technology Transfer: An Overview," *World Politics,* 31 (July 1979), pp. 539–570.

36. *Ekonomicheskaya gazeta,* no. 32 (August 1982), p. 7.

37. *Sovetskaya torgovlya,* October 12, 1982, p. 2.

38. There is a clear account of this in *Sotsialisticheskaya industriya,* February 6, 1981, p. 2.

39. John Bushnell, "The 'New Soviet Man' Turns Pessimist," in Stephen F. Cohen, Alexander Rabinowitch, and Robert Sharlet, eds., *The Soviet Union since Stalin* (Bloomington: Indiana University Press, 1980), pp. 181–182, 187.

40. Lester C. Thurow, "A Useful Mirror," *Atlantic,* February 1983, p. 102.

41. K. Chernenko, "Leninskaya strategiya rukovodstva" (The Leninist Strategy of Leadership), *Kommunist,* no. 13 (September 1981), pp. 10–11; emphasis added.

42. *Pravda,* June 16, 1983, p. 2.

43. The latest research suggests that infant mortality levelled off and began to decline in the middle to late 1970s, and also that as much as half of the increase originally reported was due to improved registration procedures, chiefly in the Moslem areas. Fred W. Grupp and Ellen Jones, "Infant Mortality Trends in the Soviet Union," *Population and Development Review,* 9 (June 1983), pp. 213–246; Murray Feshbach, "Issues in Soviet Health," in Joint Economic Committee, *Soviet Economy in the 1980s,* II, 205, 207.

44. Martha Brill Olcott, "Soviet Islam and World Revolution," *World Politics,* 34 (July 1982), p. 499.

45. Background is in Roman Solchanyk, "Russian Language and Soviet Politics," *Soviet Studies,* 34 (January 1982), pp. 23–42. The recent affirmation of the language program is in *Pravda,* May 27, 1983, p. 1.

46. Boris Rumer, "Soviet Investment Policy: Unresolved Problems," *Problems of Communism,* 31 (September-October 1982), pp. 53–68.

47. V. I. Perevedentsev, "Vosproizvodstvo naseleniya i semya" (Population Propagation and the Family), *Sotsiologicheskiye issledovaniya,* no. 2 (April-June 1982), p. 81.

Notes to Chapter 3. The Changing Soviet Elite

1. L. I. Brezhnev, *Leninskim kursom: rechi i statyi* (On the Leninist Course: Speeches and Articles) (Moscow: Politizdat, 1970–83), VIII, 115.

2. Zhores Medvedev, *Ten Years After Ivan Denisovich* (London: Macmillan, 1973), p. 46.

3. *Pravda,* August 16, 1983, p. 1.

4. Quotations from *Pravda,* August 16, 1983, p. 1, and November 23, 1982, p. 1; Yu. Andropov, "Ucheniye Karla Marksa i nekotoryye voprosy sotsialisticheskogo stroitelstva v SSSR" (Karl Marx's Teaching and Certain Problems of Socialist Development in the USSR), *Kommunist,* no. 3 (February 1983), p. 20.

5. *Pravda,* June 16, 1983, pp. 1–2.

6. Andropov, "Ucheniye Karla Marksa," p. 13.

7. Ibid.; *Pravda,* August 16, 1983, p. 1, and December 27, 1983, p. 1.

8. L. I. Brezhnev, "Glavy iz knigi 'Vospominaniya'" (Chapters from the Book *Memoirs*), *Novyi mir,* no. 1 (January 1983), p. 21.

9. Marc D. Zlotnik, "Chernenko's Platform," *Problems of Communism,* 31 (November-December 1982), p. 70.

10. Quotations from *Pravda,* February 14, 1984, pp. 1–2, and March 3, 1984, pp. 1–2.

11. Persons recently supervised by Gorbachev were made party first secretaries in the important Krasnodar and Volgograd regions (G. P. Razumovskii and Ye. I. Kalashnikov) and head of the Central Committee's chancellery (N. Ye. Kruchina).

12. V. A. Medvedev, a former Leningrad subordinate of Romanov, was made head of the Central Committee's science and education department in August 1983 (replacing an associate of Chernenko), and other Leningraders have become first deputy heads of two Central Committee departments, Deputy Foreign Minister in charge of bloc relations (B. I. Aristov), and first secretary of the relatively unimportant Vladimir party organization (R. S. Bobovikov).

13. Blair A. Ruble, "Romanov's Leningrad," *Problems of Communism,* 33 (January-February 1984), pp. 36–48.

14. This point is discussed persuasively in George W. Breslauer, *Khrushchev and Brezhnev as Leaders: Building Authority in Soviet Politics* (London: George Allen & Unwin, 1982).

15. Details on promotion from within are in Robert E. Blackwell, Jr., "Cadres Policy in the Brezhnev Era," *Problems of Communism,* 28 (March-April 1979), pp. 36–41; T. H. Rigby, "The Soviet Government since Khrushchev," *Politics,* 12 (May 1977), pp. 5–22; and T. H. Rigby, "The Soviet Regional Leadership: The Brezhnev Generation," *Slavic Review,* 37 (March 1978), pp. 13–14.

16. Of the 319 voting members of the 1981 Central Committee, only eleven had worked directly with Andropov earlier in their careers: his direct superior in the Yaroslavl region in the late 1930s (N. S. Patolichev); four individuals from the KGB (G. A. Aliyev, V. M. Chebrikov, G. K. Tsinev, and S. K. Tsvigun), the last three of whom seem to have had close ties to Brezhnev; and six associates from his days in the foreign policy establishment (G. A. Arbatov, N. N. Inozemtsev, K. V. Rusakov, L. N. Tolkunov, V. V. Zagladin, and M. V. Zimyanin). Two of these men (Tsvigun and Inozemtsev) died in

1982 before Andropov's accession. In addition, there were five persons with a more distant association from the foreign policy field, three military officers who fought on the Karelian Front in World War II, and three men with educational or work experience in the Yaroslavl or Karelia areas during Andropov's time there.

For Chernenko, only ten members of the 1981 Central Committee had a direct prior association: two from his early days in the Perm region (B. V. Konoplev and M. A. Ponomarev); three from Moldavia (I. I. Bodyul, N. A. Shchelokov, and S. P. Trapeznikov); two from his work in the Central Committee apparatus (P. F. Alekseyev and K. M. Bogolyubov); and three from Brezhnev's personal office (A. M. Aleksandrov-Agentov, K. V. Rusakov, and G. E. Tsukhanov). Four of the ten (Alekseyev, Ponomarev, Shchelokov, and Trapeznikov) were demoted under Andropov.

17. *Pravda,* November 23, 1982, p. 1.

18. The one curious fact about Ligachev is that the party second secretary in the capital city of the Tomsk region, where he served as party boss since 1965, is a certain A. K. Chernenko—evidently Konstantin Chernenko's son. This could support any number of Kremlinological theories, none of which can be explored here.

19. Former officials of Gosplan, the central planning agency, were under Andropov named national party secretary for economic planning (N. I. Ryzhkov) and heads of the Belorussian party (N. N. Slyunkov), of Soviet foreign aid (Ya. P. Ryabov), and of the construction industry (S. V. Bashilov). Several of the most prominent promotees (Ligachev, Romanov, and Vorotnikov) had backgrounds in defense production.

20. Rigby, "The Soviet Regional Leadership," pp. 23–24.

21. Of the 22 regional party first secretaries of Central Committee rank replaced under Andropov, 13 were replaced by an official from the same locality, 2 by a former local administrator most recently posted in Moscow, 2 by a person from an adjacent region, and 5 by an official from another locality. In the Council of Ministers, the pattern is less clear-cut. Of 17 new heads of USSR ministries and state committees, 7 were promotions from within the same organization, 3 from a closely related organization, and 7 from elsewhere. Of the 7 outsiders, 5 were appointed to state committees with broad duties not usually performed by professionals.

22. Grey Hodnett, "The Pattern of Leadership Politics," in Seweryn Bialer, ed., *The Domestic Context of Soviet Foreign Policy* (Boulder, Colorado: Westview Press, 1981), p. 104.

23. *Sovetskaya Rossiya,* October 10, 1967, p. 2.

24. The weakness of the wartime group is explained in Jerry F. Hough, *Soviet Leadership in Transition* (Washington, D.C.: Brookings Institution, 1980), chap. 3.

25. The clearest discussions are in ibid. (which refers to the rise of the "postwar generation") and Seweryn Bialer, *Stalin's Successors: Leadership, Stability, and Change in the Soviet Union* (Cambridge: Cambridge University Press, 1980), chap. 6 (which treats the "post-Stalin generation," defined slightly differently). Both scholars say much more about background characteristics than about shared attitudes.

26. G. A. Korotayeva and V. P. Chichkanov, "Put' na verkhnii etazh upravleniya" (The Path to the Top Floor of Management), *Ekonomika i organizatsiya promyshlennogo proizvodstva,* no. 7 (July 1981), p. 86.

27. Ibid., pp. 86–87.

28. Samuel P. Huntington, "Generations, Cycles, and Their Role in American Development," in Richard J. Samuels, ed., *Political Generations and Political Development* (Lexington, Mass.: D. C. Heath, 1977), pp. 11–12.

29. *Kazakhstanskaya pravda,* April 3, 1977, p. 4; this article is about generational differences in general, not specifically about politicians.

30. Based on analysis of the speeches as recorded in *XXVI syezd Kommunisticheskoi partii Sovetskogo Soyuza: stenograficheskii otchot* (The 26th Congress of the Communist Party of the Soviet Union: Stenographic Record) (Moscow: Politizdat, 1981). Thirteen secretaries had been born in 1926 or later and eighteen before 1926. The following are the percentages of the younger secretaries who recommended or endorsed particular types of policy in their speeches, with the percentage of older secretaries doing so in parentheses: stricter ideological controls 0 (22); extensive industrial development 15 (28); intensive industrial development 69 (50); extensive agricultural development 8 (44); intensive agricultural development 38 (28); better central management 8 (17); improved consumer welfare 62 (33); regional coordination 46 (22). A more systematic study of the published articles of regional politicians is being conducted by George W. Breslauer, with initial findings published as "Is There a Generation Gap in the Soviet Political Establishment? Demand Articulations by Provincial Party Leaders in the Russian Republic," in the January 1984 issue of *Soviet Studies.* Breslauer finds the younger secretaries to be somewhat more demanding and impatient, though he is also impressed by the diversity of outlook among them, as compared with the more uniform older group.

31. B. P. Kurashvili, "Gosudarstvennoye upravleniye narodnym khozyaistvom: perspektivy razvitiya" (State Management of the National Economy: Development Perspectives), *Sovetskoye gosudarstvo i pravo,* no. 6 (June 1982), p. 39; L. I. Abalkin, "Perevod ekonomiki na intensivnyi put' razvitiya" (Transfer of the Economy to the Intensive Path of Development), *Voprosy ekonomiki,* no. 2 (February 1982), p. 13.

32. *Ekonomicheskaya gazeta,* no. 48 (November 1981), p. 6, and no. 21 (May 1982), p. 7; *Sotsialisticheskaya industriya,* June 2, 1981, p. 2.

33. Ye. A. Lukasheva, "Sotsialno-eticheskiye problemy sotsialisticheskoi zakonnosti" (Social-Ethical Problems of Socialist Legality), *Sovetskoye gosudarstvo i pravo,* no. 4 (April 1982), pp. 15, 17.

34. G. Kh. Shakhnazarov, "Razvitiye lichnosti i sotsialisticheskii obraz zhizni" (Personal Development and the Socialist Way of Life), *Voprosy filosofii,* no. 11 (November 1977), p. 20.

35. Ustinov's praise of Andropov is in *Pravda,* May 9, 1983, p. 2.

36. On the new political organs, see *Pravda,* November 19, 1983, p. 1, and *Izvestiya,* November 25, 1983, p. 2. Two former deputy KGB chairmen were named deputies to Fedorchuk in the Interior Ministry (one of whom, V. Ya. Lezhepekov, had specialized in party work in the KGB). In addition, the new first deputy head of the Central Committee's international information department, N. N. Chetverikov, is a former KGB official. Aliyev, one of three politicians elevated to the Politburo under Andropov, was once a career KGB officer, but was a regional party boss from 1969 on.

37. Some of the possibilities for military involvement in politics at the initiative of civilians are discussed in Timothy J. Colton, *Commissars, Commanders, and Civilian Authority: The Structure of Soviet Military Politics* (Cambridge, Mass.: Harvard University Press, 1979), pp. 237–241, 250–257.

38. Many officers must have resented the promotion of Fedorchuk, who made his career in the KGB "military counterintelligence" network responsible for surveillance of the army. Peter Deriabin and T. H. Bagley, "Fedorchuk, the KGB, and the Soviet Succession," *Orbis,* 26 (Fall 1982), pp. 611–632.

39. Yu. V. Andropov, *Izbrannyye rechi i statyi* (Selected Speeches and Articles) (Moscow: Politizdat, 1979), pp. 113, 116.

40. D. Ustinov, "Istoricheskii podvig" (Historic Feat), *Kommunist,* no. 16 (November 1982), p. 27.

41. V. Kandybo. "Pravda protiv vymyslov" (The Truth versus Fabrications), *Kommunist vooruzhonnykh sil,* no. 21 (November 1982), p. 81.

42. Aspects of these overlaps are discussed in David Holloway, "War, Militarism, and the Soviet State," *Alternatives,* 6 (March 1980), pp. 59–92; and Timothy J. Colton, "The Impact of the Military on Soviet Society," in Bialer, *Domestic Context of Soviet Foreign Policy,* pp. 119–138.

43. *Pravda,* October 28, 1982, p. 1.

44. Ye. Goldberg, "Polnyeye udovletvoryat' zaprosy voinov" (To More Fully Satisfy the Troops' Concerns), *Kommunist vooruzhonnykh sil,* no. 21 (November 1982), p. 32; Ye. Goldberg, "Vysokii dolg rabotnikov voyenooi torgovli" (The Lofty Duty of Military Trade Personnel), *Tyl is snabzheniye Sovetskikh Vooruzhonnykh Sil,* no. 4 (April 1982), pp. 41–42.

Notes to Chapter 4. Reform and the Soviet Future

1. Numerous possible directions for the Soviet system are discussed in Zbigniew Brzezinski, ed., *Dilemmas of Change in Soviet Politics* (New York: Columbia University Press, 1969); George W. Breslauer, *Five Images of the Soviet Future: A Critical Review and Synthesis,* Policy Papers in International Affairs, no. 4 (Berkeley: Institute of International Affairs, University of California, 1978); and William E. Odom, "Choice and Change in Soviet Politics," *Problems of Communism,* 32 (May-June 1983), pp. 1–21.

2. Andrei Amalrik, *Will the Soviet Union Survive Until 1984?* (New York: Harper and Row, 1970).

3. The political and ethical content of the reform program is emphasized in the memoir by one of its authors, Zdeněk Mlynář, *Nightfrost in Prague* (New York: Karz Publishers, 1980).

4. K. Chernenko, "Avangardnaya rol' partii kommunistov. Vazhnoye usloviye yeyo vozrastaniya" (The Avant-Garde Role of the Community Party. An Important Condition of its Growth), *Kommunist,* no. 6 (April 1982), p. 27.

5. Quotation from Alex Pravda, "Poland 1980: From 'Premature Consumerism' to Labour Solidarity," *Soviet Studies,* 34 (April 1982), p. 168.

6. Betsy Gidwitz, "Labor Unrest in the Soviet Union," *Problems of Communism,* 31 (November-December 1982), p. 42.

7. These background factors are stressed in Roger Pethybridge, *The Social Prelude to Stalinism* (New York: St. Martin's Press, 1974); and Moshe Lewin, "The Social Background

of Stalinism," in Robert C. Tucker, ed., *Stalinism: Essays in Historical Interpretation* (New York: Norton, 1977), pp. 111–136.

8. *Pravda,* April 23, 1982, p. 2.

9. Ibid.

10. The possibility of economic re-Stalinization is considered in Joseph S. Berliner, "Managing the Soviet Economy: Alternative Models," *Problems of Communism,* 32 (January-February 1983), pp. 44–47.

11. Quotation from Grey Hodnett, "Succession Contingencies in the Soviet Union," ibid., 24 (March-April 1975), p. 21.

12. Samuel P. Huntington, "Reform and Stability in South Africa," *International Security,* 6 (Spring 1982), p. 17.

13. *Pravda,* February 1, 1983, p. 2.

14. Ibid., August 7, 1983, p. 1.

15. Quotation from ibid., August 10, 1983, p. 3.

16. See, for instance, ibid., January 23, 1984, p. 2, and January 30, 1984, p. 2.

17. Ibid., March 3, 1984, p. 2.

18. Ibid., December 27, 1983, p. 2.

19. Ibid., February 26, 1983, p. 1; March 30, 1983, p. 1; May 7, 1983, p. 1.

20. *Moskovskaya pravda,* February 5, 1983, p. 2.

21. *Pravda,* February 10, 1984, p. 1.

22. Ibid., June 16, 1983, p. 1. For a clear analysis of the background discussion, see Jerry F. Hough, "Policy-Making and the Worker," in Arcadius Kahan and Blair A. Ruble, eds., *Industrial Labor in the U.S.S.R.* (New York: Pergamon Press, 1979), pp. 367–396.

23. *Pravda,* March 3, 1984, p. 1.

24. Ibid., December 4, 1983, p. 1.

25. Ibid., February 1, 1983, p. 2.

26. Good descriptions of the main features of the reform are in Richard Portes, "The Tactics and Strategy of Economic Decentralization," *Soviet Studies,* 23 (April 1972), pp. 629–658; and David Granick, "The Hungarian Economic Reform," *World Politics,* 25 (April 1973), pp. 414–429.

27. *Pravda,* November 23, 1982, p. 1, and December 27, 1983, p. 2.

28. Excerpts from the memorandum are in *The New York Times,* August 5, 1983, p. 4. What is purported to be the full text is available in Radio Liberty, *Materialy samizdata,* no. 35/83 (August 26, 1983).

29. *Pravda,* July 26, 1983, p. 1.

30. P. G. Hare and P. T. Wanless, "Polish and Hungarian Economic Reforms—A Comparison," *Soviet Studies,* 33 (October 1981), p. 496.

31. The distinction between the two forms of planning in a Soviet-type economy is made

in Dennison Rusinow, *The Yugoslav Experiment, 1948–1974* (Berkeley: University of California Press, 1977), p. 64.

32. Huntington, "Reform and Stability in South Africa," p. 14.

33. Albert O. Hirschman, *Journeys Toward Progress: Studies of Economic Policy-Making in Latin America* (New York: Twentieth Century Fund, 1963), p. 272.

34. G. Kh. Shakhnazarov, "Razvitiye lichnosti i sotsialisticheskii obraz zhizni" (Personal Development and the Socialist Way of Life), *Voprosy filosofii,* no. 11 (November 1977), pp. 20–21.

35. *Pravda,* November 23, 1983, p. 2.

36. M. I. Piskotin, "Demokraticheskii tsentralizm: problemy sochetaniya tsentralizatsii i detsentralizatsii" (Democratic Centralism: Problems of Combining Centralization and Decentralization), *Sovetskoye gosudarstvo i pravo,* no. 5 (May 1981), p. 45.

37. David W. Paul and Maurice D. Simon, "Poland Today and Czechoslovakia 1968," *Problems of Communism,* 30 (September-October 1981), p. 31.

38. Edward A. Hewett, "The Hungarian Economy: Lessons of the 1970s and Prospects for the 1980s," in Joint Economic Committee, U.S. Congress, *East European Economic Assessment, Part 1 – Country Studies 1980* (Washington, D.C.: GPO, 1981), p. 522.

39. Huntington, "Reform and Stability in South Africa," p. 14.

Notes to Chapter 5. The Changing Soviet Union and The World

1. Yu. V. Andropov, *Izbrannyye rechi i statyi* (Selected Speeches and Articles) (Moscow: Politizdat, 1979), p. 180.

2. Alexander Dallin, "The Domestic Sources of Soviet Foreign Policy," in Seweryn Bialer, ed., *The Domestic Context of Soviet Foreign Policy* (Boulder, Colorado: Westview Press, 1981), p. 350.

3. *Pravda,* October 28, 1982, p. 1.

4. Morton Schwartz, *Soviet Perceptions of the United States* (Berkeley: University of California Press, 1978), p. 159. See also Jerry F. Hough, *Soviet Leadership in Transition* (Washington, D.C.: Brookings Institution, 1980), chap. 6.

5. *Pravda,* February 1, 1983, p. 2.

6. Adam B. Ulam, "The World Outside," in Robert F. Byrnes, ed., *After Brezhnev: Sources of Soviet Conduct in the 1980s* (Bloomington: Indiana University Press, 1983), p. 348.

7. Ibid., pp. 355–359.

8. See Dallin, p. 344–347; and Charles Gati, "The Stalinist Legacy in Soviet Foreign Policy," in Erik P. Hoffmann and Frederic J. Fleron, Jr., eds., *The Conduct of Soviet Foreign Policy* (New York: Aldine, 1980), pp. 650–656. See, by way of comparison, the statement that "significant economic reform [in the Soviet Union] is generally dependent on political and military détente, and advocacy of the two tends to go together." Jerry F. Hough, "Soviet Succession: Issues and Personalities," *Problems of Communism,* 31 (September-October 1982), p. 27.

9. *Pravda,* June 16, 1983, p. 2.

10. Ibid., November 23, 1982, p. 2. Andropov's quotation (for which he did not give a source) can be identified as Lenin's closing address at the Tenth Party Conference in May 1921, which also stated that, out of international considerations, "for us questions of economic development become of absolutely exceptional importance."

11. *Pravda,* June 16, 1983, p. 2.

12. M. A. Milshtein, "Uroki Stalingradskoi bitvy" (Lessons of the Battle of Stalingrad), *SShA: Ekonomika, politika, ideologiya,* no. 1 (January 1983), p. 15. This same note was sounded several times by Andropov—for instance in his assertion to the Central Committee following his appointment that the Soviet Union would never "request peace from the imperialists," or in his later warning that Soviet willingness to improve relations with Washington "must not be understood as a sign of weakness." *Pravda,* November 13, 1982, p. 1, and September 29, 1983, p. 1.

13. Statement from *Pravda,* June 16, 1983, p. 1.

14. Discussion in Allen S. Whiting, *Siberian Development and East Asia: Threat or Promise?* (Stanford: Stanford University Press, 1981), especially chap. 4; and Robert W. Campbell, "Prospects for Siberian Economic Development," in Donald S. Zagoria, ed., *Soviet Policy in East Asia* (New Haven: Yale University Press, 1982), pp. 229–254.

15. See on this point V. Stanley Vardys, "Polish Echoes in the Baltic," *Problems of Communism,* 32 (July-August 1983), pp. 21–34; and Martha Brill Olcott, "Soviet Islam and World Revolution," *World Politics,* 34 (July 1982), pp. 487–504. A different reading of Soviet concerns in Afghanistan can be found in Alexandre Bennigsen, "Soviet Muslims and the World of Islam," *Problems of Communism,* 29 (March-April 1980), pp. 38–51; and Eden Naby, "The Ethnic Factor in Soviet-Afghan Relations," *Asian Survey,* 22 (no. 3, 1980), pp. 237–256.

16. In the late 1970s the strategic rocket forces' share of the Soviet defense budget was less than 10 percent. Abraham Becker, "The Meaning and Measure of Soviet Military Expenditures," in Joint Economic Committee, U.S. Congress, *Soviet Economy in a Time of Change* (Washington, D.C.: GPO, 1979), I, 361.

17. *Pravda,* September 29, 1983, p. 1.

18. Gregory G. Hildebrandt, "The Dynamic Burden of Soviet Defense Spending," in Joint Economic Committee, U.S. Congress, *Soviet Economy in the 1980s: Problems and Prospects* (Washington, D.C.: GPO, 1983), I, 331–350; Daniel Bond and Herbert Levine, "The 11th Five-Year Plan, 1981–85," in Seweryn Bialer and Thane Gustafson, eds., *Russia at the Crossroads: The 26th Congress of the CPSU* (London: George Allen & Unwin, 1982), pp. 100–106, using figures for low productivity growth. Both the Hildebrandt and the Bond-Levine projections were done before the post-1977 slowdown in Soviet defense spending was known. Some guidance on this latter question can be found in Richard F. Kaufman, "Soviet Defense Trends," staff study prepared for Joint Economic Committee, U.S. Congress (Washington, D.C.: Processed, September 1983).

19. William H. Cooper, "Soviet-Western Trade," in Joint Economic Committee, *Soviet Economy in the 1980s,* I, 460.

20. Jan Vanous in *The Washington Post,* October 10, 1982, p. C5; Philip Hanson, *Trade and Technology in Soviet-Western Relations* (New York: Columbia University Press, 1981), p. 155.

21. Cooper, p. 461; Central Intelligence Agency, Office of Soviet Analysis, "USSR: Economic Trends and Policy Developments," briefing paper for Joint Economic Committee, U.S. Congress (Washington, D.C.: Processed, September 1983), p. 12.

22. Joan Parpart Zoeter, "U.S.S.R.: Hard Currency Trade and Payments," in Joint Economic Committee, *Soviet Economy in the 1980s,* II, 479–506.

23. V. Shemyatenkov, "'Ekonomicheskaya voina' ili ekonomicheskoye sorevnovaniye" ("Economic Warfare" or Economic Competition), *Mirovaya ekonomika i mezhdunarodnyye otnosheniya,* no. 3 (March 1983), p. 32.

24. O. Bogomolov, "Nauchno-tekhnicheskii progress v SSSR i yego vneshnepoliticheskiye aspekty" (Scientific-Technological Progress in the USSR and its Foreign Policy Aspects), *Planovoye khozyaistvo,* no. 4 (April 1983), p. 113.

25. Jan Vanous, "East European Economic Slowdown," *Problems of Communism,* 30 (July-August 1982), p. 4.

26. Michael Marrese and Jan Vanous, "Soviet Policy Options in Trade Relations with Eastern Europe," in Joint Economic Committee, *Soviet Economy in the 1980s,* I, 115.

27. *Pravda,* June 16, 1983, p. 2.

28. O. Bogomolov, "SEV: ekonomicheskaya strategiya 80-kh godov" (CMEA: Economic Strategy of the 1980s), *Kommunist,* no. 7 (May 1983), p. 79.

29. For example, ibid., p. 80.

30. U.S. Department of State, *Current Policy,* no. 399 (June 8, 1982), pp. 2–4.

31. The case for the slow seepage of Western cultural values into Soviet life is brilliantly made in S. Frederick Starr, *Red and Hot: The Fate of Jazz in the Soviet Union, 1917–1980* (New York: Oxford University Press, 1983).

32. George Kennan, "Breaking the Spell," *The New Yorker,* October 3, 1983, p. 53.

About the Author

Timothy J. Colton was educated at the University of Toronto and Harvard University. Since 1974 he has taught Soviet affairs and comparative government at the University of Toronto, where he is now Professor of Political Science. His publications include a book on Canadian politics and *Commissars, Commanders, and Civilian Authority: The Structure of Soviet Military Politics* (Harvard University Press, 1979). He is currently writing a book on the government and politics of the city of Moscow.